THE NAIL THAT STICKS OUT

THE NAIL THAT STICKS OUT

SUZANNE
ELKI
YOKO
HARTMANN

Reflections on the
Postwar Japanese
Canadian Community

DUNDURN
PRESS

Publisher: Meghan Macdonald | Acquiring editor: Julia Kim
Cover designer: Laura Boyle
Cover image: Kathy Hartmann

Library and Archives Canada Cataloguing in Publication

Title: The nail that sticks out : reflections on the postwar Japanese Canadian community / Suzanne Elki Yoko Hartmann.
Names: Hartmann, Suzanne Elki Yoko, author.
Description: Includes bibliographical references.
Identifiers: Canadiana (print) 20240404084 | Canadiana (ebook) 20240404130 | ISBN 9781459755048 (softcover) | ISBN 9781459755055 (PDF) | ISBN 9781459755062 (EPUB)
Subjects: LCSH: Hartmann, Suzanne Elki Yoko. | LCSH: Japanese—Ontario—Toronto— Biography. | LCSH: Toronto (Ont.)—Biography. | CSH: Japanese Canadians—Ontario— Toronto—Biography. | LCGFT: Autobiographies.
Classification: LCC FC3097.26.Y55 A3 2024 | DDC 971.3/54104092—dc23

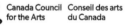

We acknowledge the support of the Canada Council for the Arts and the Ontario Arts Council for our publishing program. We also acknowledge the financial support of the Government of Ontario, through the Ontario Book Publishing Tax Credit and Ontario Creates, and the Government of Canada.

Printed and bound in Canada.

Dundurn Press
1382 Queen Street East
Toronto, Ontario, Canada M4L 1C9
dundurn.com, @dundurnpress

To Camille for insisting I write these stories
down for future generations
with special thanks to the Nakamura and Goto families,
and the Japanese Canadian community.

CONTENTS

PREFACE

LIFE IS ALWAYS in flux. In my ongoing search to uncover life's deeper meaning, I've discovered we are tied to one another in ways we don't know or understand. Often these connections aren't even apparent to us until much later, when their significance or synchronicity is revealed.

Decades ago the Toronto chapter of the National Association of Japanese Canadians (Toronto NAJC) sponsored a writing contest. This community group, which was instrumental in the fight for redress, asked contributors to share memories of Japanese Canadian (JC) community events. I wrote a reflection piece entitled "Minyō Memories," a short story about participating in *minyō* (Japanese folk dance) at Obon, an annual Buddhist summer festival. I won first place. Elated to see my story appear in the Toronto NAJC newsletter, my old friend and former dance group member Mia later confessed it was their only entry.

we never knew we had. It's time we heard a different story — one where we purge those unhealthy feelings of unworthiness and shame. When my ancestors' hopes and dreams for the future were crushed, their unwavering *gaman* (endurance), *giri* (duty), and *ganbare* (perseverance) saw them through the darkest days. These principles were etched into their psyche and continued to be passed on to the next generations. This is the Japanese way. The resilience of the issei and nisei serve as a guidepost. These first- and second-generation family and community members provide an ongoing source of pride in who we are, who we've become. This is a story of defying expectations, a triumph over adversity.

CHAPTER 1

MUKASHI, MUKASHI

MUKASHI, MUKASHI — LONG, LONG AGO. Many Japanese folk stories begin this way.

Not so long ago, there was a time when the old ways mattered. One of our traditions included a signet ring that bore our family crest. Though centuries old, this crest still identifies our family today.

Across from the large dining room table in my grandmother's condo and above a *kiku* (chrysanthemum) scroll hang two framed family crests: Nakamura and Goto. These enduring symbols are ongoing reminders of our Japanese heritage — the ties and divides between two countries, two cultures. These crests set us apart from our Japanese and Canadian peers. Each represents generations of succession lines on both sides of my mother's family tree. We've never met anyone who shares our

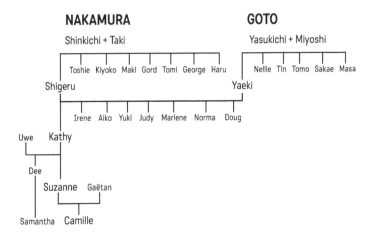

Family tree.

crest; even unrelated families with the Nakamura name have different crests. Nakamura is a common name in Japan and the kanji can be read to mean "inside the village" from *naka* (inside) and *mura* (village).

Though part of our identity, the Nakamura crest is one of those things we took for granted. No one ever spoke about its origins or how it came to represent our clan. And instead of asking important questions, I wasted so much time in my youth avoiding or fighting against my heritage. For years I lived on the offensive, tense and alert, ready to defend myself against friend, family, or foe. I remained poised and ready for battle, come what may.

Sitting at the dining room table, my one-hundred-year-old grandmother struggles to remember what happened five minutes ago. "They could come and take me away and I wouldn't know it," she says. She still has her sense of humour.

"Well, the fact that you know you're forgetting things shows you're still with it," I remind her.

It's almost dinner time and I need to start preparing our meal. When I'm visiting I like to keep her engaged with activities to focus on. I hand her the tablet that's become a fixture on the dining room table.

"Why, I never saw this before," she says, immediately engrossed in a new game of solitaire. I'm amazed at how she's taken to new technology and appears to have no trouble navigating her way around the digital device without any instructions.

Sometimes she gets stuck in a loop and repeats the same phrase or story again and again. It used to bother me when she first started to do this and I was quick to say something. Now I just let her talk it through. I'm happy to hear her voice and spend this time with her once a week on the afternoon shift. Between two personal support worker (PSW) shifts, one during the day and another overnight, our family fills the gaps to ensure Grandma is never alone.

The small formalities we've grown up with are so imprinted on us. Grandma always makes a point of thanking me, whether it's for making dinner, getting the tea, cleaning up, or helping her into her pyjamas. We often laugh together at this irony, how our roles have reversed after all these years. "I'm just returning the favour," I tell her.

We remain hunkered down at the dining room table after dinner to attend to "the business." Even at her advanced age, she remains a competitive rummy tiles player, particularly when there are stakes involved. She swears it keeps her brain active. All that counting, adding, and strategically matching suits, sets, and runs. Any novice is soon parted from their money.

"The night PSW will be here soon," I remind her.

"You think after all this time, I could remember her name. I'm getting so lost," she confesses with a sigh. "Things are fading away. Some things you can't forget. Sad, bad things you try not to remember. Try to remember the good times. It helps."

She continues to amaze me with her wisdom and insight. Despite her failing short-term memory, my grandmother is still lucid, still the family storyteller and keeper of lore and secrets.

Who will tell our stories when she's gone? It's heartbreaking when I think, *She's slowly slipping away.* I try to remain cheerful, to cherish these moments together as if they are our last.

"We never know when it's our time."

Despite how many times I've heard her say this, I'm quick to push these thoughts away, not wanting to envision a future without her. I'm just grateful she's still here.

• • •

As children we heard different narratives: some true, others false. In our innocence we accepted them, however narrow or imposed. Later, as we learned to discern fact from fiction, questions arose: Are we merely clinging to symbols of the past? What versions of the story are real or imagined? Poking holes into the dark fabric of the unknown, we weigh each probability. We're not always prepared for what we discover when the facts don't align in our ongoing quest for the truth.

The Dobersteins lived next door to the Nakamura family on Browning Avenue in Toronto. The older couple converted their home into a rooming house and in the early 1960s welcomed a young German immigrant named Uwe Hartmann. The Nakamuras mistook him for a military man and remembered how he used to walk with the upright and precise gait of men in uniform. Uwe carried himself with confidence and

A 1960s Polaroid of Kathy and Uwe — a rare photo of them together.

quickly garnered the attention of his neighbour's oldest daughter, Kathy Nakamura.

Attracted by differences that later divided them, Kathy married outside of her culture. Although Kathy's parents were always warm and welcoming to Uwe, there might have been an underlying shame. Once the young couple's biracial children were born, there was no hiding their features. As one of those kids, I often felt we were tolerated by the Japanese Canadian (JC) community out of respect for my mother's family. Among JCs we were instantly recognized as not quite

Japanese; everywhere else it was clear we weren't fully white. Standing out in this way provided an early education on the pain of exclusion. My mother's family encouraged resilience and built me up with the Canadian dream — to believe I could be anything, do anything — only to later crush me down and rein in my ambitions with the yoke of Japanese cultural traditions. Years of carrying that burden ignited a burning fire that was slow to subside.

Though my father disappeared before early childhood memories formed, another man was already there to take his place. Reserved and straitlaced, my Japanese grandfather embodied family values through his living example. Looking back I appreciate how he was a pioneer in his own right. After he retired he made a statement by venturing into no man's land — the kitchen — and learned how to run the dishwasher and use the microwave to heat up snacks for his visiting grandchild. My grandmother berated him for indulging me in my defiant and independent ways when he hardly had time for his own children. She instructed me to make better use of my time and energy by staying home and learning how to cook and sew.

• • •

Generations of living in Canada eroded our connection to the Nakamura family in Japan. My ancestors toiled as early settlers in the Canadian wilderness, struggling to gain their footing in a foreign country. Early days filled with hard living and many mouths to feed helped stoke the fires of a warrior spirit infused with incredible endurance.

I didn't know my great-grandfather Shinkichi Nakamura. He died during a return trip to Japan in 1938 when my grandfather was still a young man. Shinkichi was the second youngest of six children. In Japanese tradition only the eldest son inherited the family homestead, so the other children needed to seek their livelihoods elsewhere. Many Japanese thought they'd make their fortune in Canada and abroad. Details such as when and where Shinkichi arrived in North America are unclear, and his passage records remain elusive. Family members say he immigrated to the U.S. around 1898 as an eighteen-year-old and did odd jobs like cooking and cleaning while studying in the Seattle area. Other accounts had him working in the kitchens for the U.S. Navy and sailing along the Pacific coast to Hawaii and back. Uncle George, in his self-published family account, *The Nakamura Legacy*, recalled his father jumping from a merchant marine ship somewhere near Oregon. From there he made his way to Seattle and eventually crossed the border as an illegal immigrant into British Columbia, where he settled, married, and started a family.

Shinkichi's wife, Taki — my great-grandmother, whom we called Bāchan — was a constant presence in my childhood. Shinkichi and Taki had eight children. The number eight has always been considered lucky in our family. My grandfather Shigeru was their eldest son and married my grandmother Yaeki Goto. He and my grandmother also had eight children of their own. My mother, Kathy, is their eldest.

After Bāchan died in November 1980, Grandpa and Grandma decided to return to Japan in the new year to retrieve Shinkichi's remains and bury them with Taki in Canada. During the trip my grandparents visited Hakone, a scenic town located west of Tokyo and famous for its views of Mount Fuji. One day they ventured into a museum filled with samurai artifacts, and in one of the glass cabinets, Grandpa happened

Grandpa as a handsome young man in his 1946 passport photo.

on a display of samurai helmets, or *kabuto*. Right away the Nakamura crest caught his eye. Perhaps, like me, he never had the chance to ask his father about its history.

Crests, called *kamon* or *mon* for short, were created as symbols of power and continue to serve as family emblems. Samurai and nobility adopted these identifiers to reflect their family lineage. They proudly displayed them on flags, swords, and armoury to easily identify and distinguish between warring groups on the battlefield. This trend later spread to other classes who sought their own, although there was an unspoken rule against using another family's crest. *Mon* were later used to mark merchant carts, shops, merchandise, ships, and gravesites. My grandfather always wore a gold ring stamped with the family *mon*. He and his brothers had them specially made. His youngest brother, George, like some Japanese families, filed for copyright on the symbol and for years used it as the logo for his business.

Curious to know more, Grandpa wrote to the museum's curator and inquired about the origins of the item. Grandma doesn't remember the specifics, but it likely was the Hakone Mononofuno Sato Art Museum. Prominently displayed on their website, among the collection of samurai artifacts from the Muromachi to Edo periods, is the Takeda clan crest. In the curator's response, translated by Yasuko Nishimura,[1] Grandpa learned some of the exhibited materials were purchased from a local antiques dealer when the museum opened in 1965. Detailed explanations were absent, but museum staff speculated items such as the *kabuto* were worn by samurai during formal occasions during the Edo period under the Tokugawa shogunate.

The curator also indicated our Nakamura crest originated from the Satake clan. Their crest is almost identical to ours, but it differs in how the fan is presented. The Satake's five-bone fan features a prominent opaque sun, whereas the Nakamura crest, called *maru no ōgi*, has an unembellished fan enclosed within a circle. In other records the curator consulted, the Nakamura family name originated with a warrior named Nobusada Itagaki. His son, Kanekuni, was the first to use the Nakamura name. Nobusada was a Takeda clan retainer providing military services and a descendant of Kanenobu Itagaki, who as one of the Takeda brothers, started this branch of his clan during the Takeda regime.

Between this ancient history and the present lies a vast expanse clouded by time and separation, two continents, and a lost language. Whether these Satake, Takeda, or Itagaki families were distant ancestors remains unknown. Somewhere in Japan, old family registry documents called *koseki* may reveal what has long been forgotten. Although I was excited to discover this information and the curator's letter to Grandpa, without Japanese literacy skills, I was unable to verify these and other sources on my own. I realized I may never know the full extent of these historical accounts and have taken them with a grain of salt.

Early Japanese history is complex. Despite Japan's diminutive size compared to Canada, the country's islands were divided into various territories ruled by large clans. Some of these families were related and formed alliances with others, while bitter rivals fought against one another in their desire to seize power and control. It's easy to imagine the thunder of horses galloping across a battlefield in the northern provinces as General Yoritomo Minamoto rode his trusty steed. Legend has it, on July 21, 1189, when surveying his supporters' troops, Minamoto noticed one clan carried a white flag similar to his own. In a display of thanks for this loyalty, he decided to mark the occasion by presenting the *ōgi ni tsuki-maru*, or rising sun with five-bone fan crest, to their leader, Hideyoshi Satake. From that day on, the Satake[2] clan adopted the symbol on that historic battle flag as their family crest. With these alliances, Minamoto continued his rise to power and in 1192 became Japan's first *shōgun* and established their system of military government.

• • •

Once I graduated from university, instead of a school ring, it seemed natural to want a family crest ring. To me the *mon* represented a familial bond, a reflection of our ancestry and extensive cultural heritage — a physical reminder of my debt to family and a link to the past — wherever the future might take me.

Tradition being what it was, Grandma simply stated, "These things are not for girls." She said I would eventually marry and become part of my husband's family and no longer be one of them. After hearing her words, I no longer wanted to be part of the family. The ties that bind now strangulated. My mother was taken aback by my bold request but turned away, refusing to comment on the matter.

"Ohhh, we didn't know you were such a feminist," one aunt said.

"Why would you want the ring? Surely you would be happier with a pendant necklace or charm bracelet — that's what the aunties have," another aunt said.

For me it was a matter of principle, no halfway measures. All or nothing. If that had been the end of it, I might have accepted their decision and moved on. Instead, a new family tradition emerged when the first grandson was presented with a family crest ring when he graduated, a trend enjoyed by most of the other grandsons. It's hard to be gracious when faced with old inequities, aggravating a wound that never quite healed. Years later I discovered other branches of our extended family were not bound to these old ways. My grandfather's siblings took a different approach as evidenced by my female cousins wearing their own family crest rings.

My grandfather remained firm in his opinion: only those who bore the Nakamura name were entitled to use his crest. He disagreed with Grandma's double standard but knew better than to argue with her. Out of respect no one challenged my grandmother or my great-grandmother before her. Inside the home they were the authority, their words were law. They may have remained mum outside the home, but inside, the women reigned as keepers of the keys in prisons not of their design. They knew their place and stayed in it. Instead of breaking free from the bondage of the past, these women chose to pursue their "freedom within the form" — living within a set of parameters — and perpetuated this outdated ideology by firmly impressing it on the generations that came after.

One time, fearing he had lost his ring, Grandpa swore me to secrecy, saying "there would be big trouble" if the women knew. Apparently, it had gone missing before and the family had torn the house apart in a frantic search. "All for a silly ring — not even worth that much money." Trying to help, I asked, "When did you have it last? Where were you? What were you wearing?"

Mulling this over, he walked toward the clothes rack and began rifling through his suit pockets. Perhaps his ring was never really missing but stashed in his vest pocket all along. Pulling it out, he mused, "Who would want?"

"Everyone," I said. "Just because it's yours." Following his example, we always spoke plainly.

After a pause he turned to me with the ring in his outstretched hand and asked, "You want?"

A tsunami of emotion washed over me as a million thoughts raced through my mind. *Had my moment of recognition finally arrived? Was he testing me? How would the family react? Would they say I took advantage of a feeble old man?* Rising and subsiding, my hopes soared and then crashed. Something so cherished and anticipated slowly diminished. I could only turn away and withdraw. Instead, I told him what he already knew — the rules of succession. "They'll bury you with it before they let anyone else have it," I sighed.

To this day I'm not entirely sure what his intentions were. An image of us standing silently in Bāchan's old room remains frozen in my mind. We shared an understanding and connection in that moment, an eternity.

• • •

I was not with my grandfather when he passed, but somehow I felt I knew when he went. He had fallen ill and died at age ninety-four. Driving Grandma to visit him each week had become our routine. First we went to the hospital and months later to the palliative care centre. I tried to be animated during our visits but found it disheartening to see the dignified man I loved struggle against the indignities of old age and decline.

Reluctantly, I tore myself away, and with my husband, Gaëtan, and child, Camille, decamped to my mom's place in

him to depart on April Fools' Day. Grandpa loved his practical jokes, and many family members thought this was his final jest. Few people outside the family would have guessed behind his direct, deadpan demeanour hid a wry sense of humour. How I miss that old man! He seemed to delight in seeing me pushing back against expectations — charging ahead at full speed and miles away from the cage of quiet obedience. Never one to flatter or condescend, he remained proud and unwavering to the very end, steadfast and sincere in ways that spoke volumes of words never said.

Setting out early in the morning with my dog, Ivy, we took our usual detour through the wooded area in a nearby park. Scrambling up tree roots to reach the top of the hill, we paused for a moment. Suddenly, a large overhead shadow startled me. At first I mistook the feathered friend for an owl, but when we saw the huge bird again, I determined it was more likely a hawk. Facing us, it circled the trees along the perimeter of the baseball diamond before landing in a clump of trees. From our vantage point in the dog run, I watched the hawk with wonder. I've always been fascinated by encounters with wild animals. Some view these occasions as omens. For Japanese, hawks were prized by samurai and represented power. It's not unusual to see men's kimono feature hawk designs on their fabric. These birds have appeared in all types of mythology and are generally considered a symbol of freedom and a divine messenger.

In an announcement later that day, Toronto mayor John Tory proclaimed April 1, 2021, to be Japanese Canadian Freedom Day in the city. Part of the proclamation, posted on Facebook, read as follows:

On April 1, 1949, Canadian citizens of Japanese ancestry were given the right to vote and the freedom to live anywhere in Canada.

Today is a day to acknowledge the contributions of the Japanese Canadian community to the City of Toronto while recognizing the difficult path to belonging faced by generations of Japanese Canadians.

The City of Toronto is committed to promoting fundamental human rights and is working to address all forms of discrimination and stand up against hatred, intolerance and discrimination.[3]

Clearly, Grandpa is still watching over us.

CHAPTER 2

THE KIMONO

EVERY YEAR, AS a buildup to *Oshogatsu,* or what we call New Year's Day, it's a Japanese custom to do some rigorous housecleaning. This noble goal of getting one's home in order is believed to bring good luck for the year ahead. Growing up surrounded by unadmitted hoarders, I've tried to counteract the clutter. Clearing the bedroom closets one year, I came across a kimono made by my great-grandmother Taki Nakamura, our family founder on my mother's side. I had been fortunate to know her. She was my grandfather's mother — Bāchan as everyone called her.

Finding the kimono took me back to my childhood, living with my parents on the third floor of my grandparents' home in Toronto's Greektown. Bought in 1955, the house on Browning Avenue was a large turn-of-the-century semi, not quite Edwardian or fully Victorian in style but always bustling with family and friends. Like many multigenerational homes, it housed countless family members who came and went. Bāchan remained a permanent fixture.

At the time of Bāchan's death in 1980, the kimono was one of the few items no one wanted and so it was given to me, a teenager who loved vintage things. Decades later I marvelled at the memories it contained. It wasn't your classic silk kimono. No, it was a rather plain house kimono called *nemaki*. For sleeping attire Bāchan never opted for pyjamas or housecoats but preferred traditional Japanese kimono. What struck me was the heavy weave, a dark brown fabric with dotted stripes — the strong yet subdued dress of older women and not the bright colours worn by the young. In all likelihood it was made from material leftover from a *futon* (quilt), *zabuton* (cushion), or other sewing project.

In Japan Bāchan's family kept silkworms, so she was knowledgeable about textiles and a talented crafter. In those days a young girl prepared for her future by assembling an entire wardrobe. Once she married this cache of clothing ensured the young bride had ample items to wear in the years ahead. Bāchan continued to sew long into her eighties, although by then her failing eyesight meant someone else had to thread the sewing machine for her. I don't believe she ever owned a pair of pants. True to her time, she wore mostly formal clothing and wouldn't leave the house without her hat and gloves.

When I knew her, she lived in my grandparent's home and had a room of her own on the second floor. As the long-time matriarch of the family, Bāchan was the authority on how things were done and never lost her ability to issue orders instead of simply asking. To her grandchildren, though, Bāchan

Bāchan with her great-grandchildren in the late 1960s.

was different. She always had a smile and an endless supply of hard candies. On many occasions she delighted in entertaining us. She'd laugh as she performed her famous trick of juggling several beanbags in one hand.

Like many immigrants Bāchan never learned to speak English in her ninety-plus years despite living in Canada longer than she had in Japan. The Second World War effectively created unseen barriers between generations. Learning to speak Japanese is difficult at best and was further hampered by limited educational resources during incarceration. After the war the family moved east from Slocan, British Columbia, to Chatham, Ontario, before settling in downtown Toronto in 1947. As they began to reestablish themselves in an unfamiliar city, the pressure to assimilate resulted in my mother's generation losing their heritage language. People like my great-grandmother were effectively silenced from sharing their stories and folklore.

In my own attempts to learn Japanese, I discovered the language I knew from home was not the current and evolved language of Japan but an obsolete version rooted in the past — often mispronounced and misspelt. For example, most JCs know *obāsan* is the formal Japanese word for "grandmother" and *bāchan* an informal version of "grandma." We grew up seeing it spelled *bachan*, without the macron above the first *a* to indicate the long vowel, that additional "ah" sound in *baachan*. The things we never knew.

Often we remember things as being larger than they are, and when we encounter them later in life, we're surprised at what we find. When I held up the old kimono, I was shocked at how small it was. Most kimono are one-size-fits-all with an abundance of material. But not this one. It was old and fragile yet strong and sturdy. It personified Bāchan: a tiny woman with a will of iron forged from earlier days as a Canadian pioneer. Perhaps it was a blessing she was so petite, for at four-foot seven-inches tall, she didn't need much fabric.

The reality of her life was worlds away from the life she expected to live. Born on Oshima Island in Japan's Yamaguchi prefecture in February 1889, Taki Kinoshita grew up in a wealthy family, educated and pampered by servants. When hard times hit, her parents arranged her marriage and Taki set sail for Canada with high hopes for a new life as a "picture

bride." Little did she know when she stepped off the boat
in January 1909 to meet my great-grandfather Shinkichi
Nakamura she was headed for a one-room shack on a farm in
Port Hammond, British Columbia.

Bound for Seattle, Washington, the SS *Kaga Maru* departed
from China before reaching Japan via Yokohama on December
23, 1908. Handwritten in dark cursive, Taki's name and details
appear among nine other Japanese passengers, with their ultimate destination marked as Vancouver. Searching for definitive
details about the carrier, I discovered different sources listed
different information. Another ship matched the timeline and
had a similar name — the *Kagi Maru*, built in 1907. Did the
handwritten document contain a typo? To complicate matters,
these sources had conflicting dates for when the *Kaga Maru*
was built. The Ships List website reports it was built in 1901
and then scrapped in 1934 at Yokohama, but it listed two other
ships with the same name built later. Which one was right?
The *Japanese Merchant Ships Recognition Handbook*[1] solved the
mystery by stating it was customary for Japanese to give multiple vessels the same name though they differed in size and
appearance. *Maru* usually means "circle" in Japanese but was
added to the names of ships as a term of endearment.

Unlike the picture brides Julie Otsuka describes in *The
Buddha in the Attic*,[2] who slept in dim and filthy lower-level
steerage, Taki and the other Japanese travelled comfortably
in first class, except for one servant assigned to a second-class
cabin. Curiously, the forty passengers in steerage were all
Europeans. Once they reached their destination, a cruel rever-
sal awaited the Japanese passengers. For people like Taki, who
had known wealth and status and expected to begin a better
life in a new country, this voyage to North America provided a

different experience — in Canada they were reduced to lowly peasants, scorned, discriminated against, and viewed with suspicion by the white majority.

In *The Enemy That Never Was*,[3] Ken Adachi writes of how growing resentments toward Asian immigrants as a "yellow horde" or "yellow peril" plagued Vancouver and led to the race riots in September 1907. But by 1908, the arrival of many picture brides like Bāchan marked the beginning of a new chapter in this family-and-community-building stage. The influx of wives and birth of children slowly transformed the male-dominated environment of transient workers, stabilizing the community and rooting the Japanese in Canada.

No one in our family knew the original details about Bāchan's arrival. Several online searches yielded no insights, which puzzled me. Originally, I thought she embarked on her journey as a young, unmarried woman travelling to meet her future husband. When I finally found the passage record, her name was listed with my great-grandfather's surname. Adachi's extensive history on JCs again provided the missing puzzle piece. Prior to an arranged marriage, parents or relatives in Japan undertook extensive searches to locate a suitable mate before the eventual exchange of photos or letters between a prospective bride and groom. Once the couple or their family agreed to the union, the marriage was registered in Japan — a simple matter of affixing the man's seal on the required document and presenting it to the registrar. Picture brides like Bāchan were married on paper before ever meeting their groom.[4]

Another detail bothered me. Although Taki's twenty-first birthday had been weeks away, someone at the Land Registry Office in Victoria took the liberty of rounding up her age and listed the twenty-one-year-old "spinster" as marrying a twenty-eight-year-old bachelor and farmer. Thankfully, record-keeping isn't what it used to be.

• • •

In a yellowing black-and-white wedding photo, a white flower is attached to the lapel of Shinkichi Nakamura's three-piece suit. Taki, hair swept off her face and tucked under a large, black-brimmed hat, wears a prim white shirt with puffy blouson sleeves, tightly buttoned around the neck and tucked into a dark, pleated, full-length skirt. After meeting in Vancouver, the two Buddhists made their way to Victoria. They headed to the Oriental Home and School (OHS) at 724 Cormorant Street, where Rev. A.E. Robertson performed their wedding service on January 12, 1909.

This new facility had just opened in December 1908, and the welcoming place included social space and other facilities to help meet the growing needs of the community: "The Oriental Home and School offered shelter and Christian education for Chinese and Japanese women, girls and children. The OHS operated a Sunday school, encouraged marriage to Christian Asian men, conducted Canadian marriage ceremonies, found job placements in Christian homes, and generally fostered 'white middle-class values.' It remained closely affiliated with Metropolitan Methodist/United Church."[5] Originally established on the same street in 1888 by Chinese-born missionary John Endicott Gardner from the United Church with support from Rev. J.E. Starr, the OHS was later joined by the Women's Missionary Society, part of the Pandora Avenue Methodist Church. While this was Taki's first introduction to the

United Church in Canada, she later converted to Christianity, and once she moved to Toronto, she faithfully attended the Centennial-Japanese United Church on Dovercourt Road.

Within their first year of marriage, Shinkichi and Taki lost everything when their log cabin burnt to the ground. Undeterred, they carried on and by 1910 my grandfather Shigeru was born in Port Hammond. Work in a railway tie mill prompted a move to Strawberry Hill in Surrey. On a small plot located on Gibson Road, Shinkichi built the community's first log cabin, and like other Japanese farmers in the area, the couple raised chickens and grew strawberries.

As the family grew, Taki and Shinkichi wanted their children to have a proper Japanese education. Not far away in Vancouver's Japantown, the Japanese community had already constructed the Vancouver Japanese Language School in 1906, but it was a different story in rural Strawberry Hill. Shinkichi likely reached out to his older sister to make arrangements. Kiyo Yanagihara lived alone in Japan after both her husband and son had died tragically of some illness. She lived on Oshima Island in Yamaguchi prefecture and welcomed any help she could get managing the family silk farm. Like other families without heirs, she legally adopted her brother in 1919 and he changed his surname to her married name. However, this was likely a guardianship formality so three of his children could study abroad.

While Shinkichi stayed behind to manage the homestead, Taki boarded a ship to Japan on November 18, 1918, with my grandfather Shigeru (8) and his two sisters, Toshie (4) and Kiyoko (1) — leaving the city of Vancouver behind in full Armistice Day celebration mode. After several months Taki returned to Canada alone on July 6, 1919. Her children were left in the care of Aunt Kiyo and used Yanagihara as their last name. When not attending school or engaged in their studies, they earned their keep by cutting mulberry branches for the silk-worms to eat and helped sell the harvested cocoons at market.

Back at the Strawberry Hill farm in Canada, three more children were born: Maki, Gord, and Tomi. Shinkichi continued to work at the mill and became friends with a Mr. Harrow, who later moved to Salt Spring Island and encouraged the family to follow him. In 1924 the Nakamuras exchanged one pastoral setting for another and settled on the island in the town of Ganges. They took over a laundry business in addition to woodcutting and farming strawberries and vegetables. There the last of their eight children (George and Haru) were born.

One of the earliest photos of the Nakamura family, Salt Spring Island, 1928. From left: Tomi, Taki, Shigeru, Gord, Shinkichi with baby George, and Maki.

With a large family and limited income, Taki became a practical and thrifty homemaker but never lost her taste for small luxuries, like soft cotton. Rice, flour, and sugar used to be packaged in large cotton sacks, and like many other people, she resourcefully salvaged the fabric. A closer look at the kimono tells volumes of these early years, particularly the faded pink cotton yoke, black hems on the armhole sleeves, and solid brown accents on the collar ends — all scraps of material but expertly sewn.

About six years after his departure, young Shigeru made the voyage back to Canada in May 1924 aboard the SS *Alabama*. Once in Canada he reverted to using the Nakamura surname. His transition to speaking English proved difficult, so the fourteen-year-old stayed in Vancouver for a while, working in a local *senbei* (rice cracker) shop during the day and taking English classes at night. Shigeru's sisters remained in Japan until Aunt Kiyo died (what happened to the Yanagihara homestead is uncertain). Returning in June 1930 on the *Arabia-Maru*, the girls faced a short holdup during immigration. Records indicated the Nakamura children departed, yet there were two Japanese-speaking girls dressed in traditional kimono listed as Yanagihara on the passenger list. How could they claim to be Canadians? After they spent a few harrowing days in detention, Taki rushed in to claim the girls and they were reunited with the family.

With Shigeru and his sisters back from Japan, the small, crowded rental in Ganges now housed all ten family members. The two oldest sisters didn't remain for long. Both managed to secure work with room and board. Once employed they were encouraged to settle down by their parents. Arranged marriages followed and the sisters started families of their own soon after.

Toshie, the oldest daughter, worked as a housemaid, improving her English before landing a position in a converted farmhouse called the Harbour House Hotel. She married in 1935. Kiyoko worked as a live-in housekeeper for Mrs. Best, an Anglican Sunday school teacher who converted her to Christianity. Kiyoko married in the fall of 1938. Curiously, Yanagihara is listed as her last name on her wedding registration.

Their father, Shinkichi, fell ill with throat cancer. He could no longer eat solid foods and needed to use a feeding tube in his stomach. Despite his poor health, he made a solo journey back to Japan in 1938. Whether he wanted to pay his respects after a forty-year absence or return to his familiar homestead as a final resting place, he succumbed to the disease while in Japan and was buried in the Nakamura family plot. Taki was now a widow with young children. Traditionally, the family patriarch managed family affairs and a father's absence or death signalled the informal transfer of responsibility to the eldest son. Now entrusted with the family's welfare and responsible for his younger siblings, Shigeru became the head of the clan. He sent what money he could to Japan to help with the funeral and burial costs.

My grandfather Shigeru knew how the family business operated. He'd worked with his father at Snow White Laundry and Agincourt Farms, earning enough money to buy a Model T. At age twenty-eight, he remained a bachelor. He may have been one of the first JCs in the area to own a car, but managing the duties of a large family was an entirely different matter. A family friend stepped in as the go-between and made introductions between Taki and the Goto family at their Gibson Road farm in the Sunbury area of Delta, British Columbia, to discuss an arranged marriage. Two years later, in a January 1940 service officiated by Rev. Gordon Nakayama, Shigeru married Yaeki Goto. The bride was the eldest of the Gotos' six children and no stranger to hard work. Despite being only twenty years old and eleven years younger than the groom, Yaeki was well-versed in running a household and considered an asset to the Nakamura family.

Decades later, when the grandchildren asked how the couple met, a sly smile would appear on Grandpa's face. In his halting English, he told the story of an earlier visit to the Strawberry Hill neighbourhood. To save time he decided to take a shortcut off the main route. These actions proved serendipitous as he walked into a clearing. For there, beside an unfamiliar family farmstead, he spotted what he could only describe as the most beautiful maiden he had ever seen, hanging laundry. Immediately smitten, he rushed to make the necessary arrangements. Grandma's version of events always seemed devoid of the romanticism Grandpa infused into his recollections. When she told the story, with a matter-of-fact emphasis, she maintained it was not her whom Grandpa spotted on that fateful day. While she certainly had her share of chores, apparently one of her sisters always did the laundry. But since she was the oldest, she had to be the first to go.

Thus, another era began. Once her grandchildren were born, Bāchan's role expanded to overseer of a whole new generation. By chance the Sawada family, relatives of family friend Kiyo Ise, decided to return home to Japan and were looking for someone to take over their dry cleaning business in Victoria. With high hopes and funds scraped together, the Nakamuras island-hopped over to Victoria, ready to start afresh. Nothing could have prepared them for the fate that awaited them.

• • •

My memories, both happy and sad, flood back in waves. In one light the kimono is solemn and understated; in another, shabby and worn. I was alarmed when I noticed several small holes in the fabric. Were there moths in the closets? On closer examination I ascertained they were burn holes. Though hard to fathom today, Bāchan started smoking as a young girl back in Japan. Apparently, an ever-lit pipe was set out in one of the rooms, and in between playing with her dolls, Bāchan used to sneak in and take a few puffs.

Some images are forever etched in our minds. For me it's my grandparents' kitchen on Browning Avenue. The main floor contained three large rooms with ten-foot-high ceilings. The front living room had wooden pocket doors opening into the wood-panelled dining room, and the adjacent galley-style kitchen was positioned at the back of the home. Behind the kitchen and the dining room was a small pantry. Latched cupboards packed with food staples lined the walls, and an extra refrigerator blocked the swing door access to the dining room.

In the kitchen a long Arborite table sat centre stage and was pushed up against the wood-panelled wall outside of mealtimes. Flanking its sides were mismatched chairs and a long bench. Grandpa's chair sat at the head of the table and Bāchan's bench presided at the other end. Custom-made by Grandpa in his basement workshop, the small wooden bench sported bright red legs and a blue vinyl seat. I remember Bāchan sitting there Japanese-style, legs tucked underneath, and a green-and-white Macdonalds Tobacco tin drum and cigarette papers stacked beside her on the table. Carefully, she rolled sausage-like cigarettes, which burnt off excess paper when lit, creating what looked like a flash of fire. After a few quick puffs, huge clouds of smoke engulfed her entire head. Sometimes she even blew a

In the kitchen on Browning Avenue with Bāchan, Easter 1978.

smoke ring or two with a laugh to amuse us before she stubbed out the cigarette.

In her nineties Bāchan became ill. I remember visiting her a few times in the hospital with my mom and grandmother. On one occasion we were filled with alarm when greeted by an empty bed. Standing under the fluorescent lights beside the litter of sheets, we heard a clamour of voices behind us. We turned to see two of her kids, my great-aunts, rolling her into the room giggling and reeking of smoke. They had snuck her into the bathroom to smoke their store-bought cigarettes.

Sadly, Bāchan never recovered but succumbed to pneumonia in November 1980 at age ninety-one. A year later Grandma and Grandpa trekked to Japan to retrieve Shinkichi's remains, and my great-grandparents were reunited in Toronto's Highland Memorial Gardens cemetery.

• • •

Laying the kimono flat on my bed, I began folding it into sections, as I had been taught to do during my odori days, when my young child, Camille, suddenly bounced in and immediately asked to wear the kimono for Halloween.

"You can borrow one of my old ones," I suggested. "Let's go look and see what we can find. Bāchan's kimono I'm preserving for the future, for your children's children."

If a picture can represent a thousand words, perhaps a kimono can offer a glimpse into a life long past. The fabric of Bāchan's life held fast between those strands and fibres so others might know the matriarch who came before them and share through each woven thread her joys and sorrows, her sacrifices and gains.

CHAPTER 3

LEAVING HOME

THERE WERE NO tears when we parted that August 2019 afternoon in Santa Clarita, California. After goodbye hugs, my husband and I sat in the rental car. We watched Camille walk up and over the hill, disappearing into the trees and shrubs surrounding Chouinard Hall, the undergrad residence and orientation hub at California Institute of the Arts (CalArts), where we had picked up keys earlier that morning. We waited for a short while, reluctant to leave just in case Camille had a change of heart. I would have been happy for us to spend one last night together at the hotel. In my mind's eye, I imagined our child turning and sprinting back to the car.

For two freshly hatched empty nesters, it was a quiet drive back to Burbank. Our only child had finally spread their wings and flown far away from home. But in this mad dash to get everything ready, we still needed time to catch our breath. Back at the hotel, we found ourselves with time on our hands and decided to step out for a bite. Wandering down the road, we happened on a nearby diner. Peering in, we noticed it appeared to cater to older adults.

"It can't be that bad, not with so many people inside," I suggested. We took our chances and ventured in. Sitting in one of the vinyl booths, we soon became steeped in nostalgia by the background music. We hummed along to classic songs we knew practically every word to. Our conversation surrounding the day's events was punctuated by one of us singing the odd line from an eighties punk or new wave hit. We found ourselves in a sentimental mood, transported back in time and revisiting memories of our own school days. We paid the bill and strolled back to the hotel, laughing when it occurred to us — we fit right in with the rest of the diner's clientele. The restaurant catered to our generation. Somewhere along the road, we'd aged.

Our whirlwind tour started the day before in Toronto, and when the three of us landed at Los Angeles International Airport (LAX), the adventure had just begun. It was a journey in itself to find the rental car building and then our hotel in Burbank, where we dropped our bags before making our way to Ikea that evening. Our to-do list was long with no plans for leisure. This was no holiday; there was too much to do.

We took an early dinner break before tackling more shopping and marvelled at the picturesque vistas that greeted us. Through floor-to-ceiling windows in Ikea's dining area, the setting sun cast a warm glow over the surrounding mountains. Were we really in California? Was it just a dream? After coffee and breakfast the next morning, we squeezed into the car, jam-packed with the accoutrements of Camille's new life, and headed up Interstate 5-North. About half an hour later, we stopped to check in at the security gate of the renowned CalArts. We had officially arrived. A beautiful backdrop awaited and a whole new story set to begin.

When Camille began researching grad schools, we'd never heard of CalArts. Known among Hollywood insiders, the private university was founded in 1961 by Walt Disney and his brother Roy when they merged the Chouinard Art Institute and the Los Angeles Conservatory of Music. For an artist and a musician like Camille, it seemed a perfect fit. The main hitch? The location — thousands of miles away from home, on the other side of the continent, and south of the border. And another thing: the hefty price tag. Even without the conversion rate we faced, we wondered how any American could afford education.

None of us had ever been to LA, so we had no idea where the school was located or what to expect. Camille had forgone the in-person audition, not wanting us to incur the steep travel expenses. Plus it was no guarantee of acceptance. Someone in admissions had suggested, "Save your money." We took the sound advice. Once the application and portfolio were submitted, excitement in our house started to build. Someone in California was spending hours listening to the music links Camille provided on SoundCloud. The day the letter of acceptance arrived, Camille, in a state of euphoria, could hardly believe the good news. Was it really true? To us, it was no surprise. Our honour student worked hard to get there and had a long track record of academic and musical awards to show for it.

"You need to build a cabinet or an award room for all of Camille's medals!" my mother joked with each accolade. Who knew the Royal Conservatory of Music gave out gold awards? I almost deleted the email when Camille first won years ago.

I thought it was spam, and the newspaper had to quote me on this when they interviewed us. Even neighbours sent their congratulations after they saw the article and Camille's photo in the local paper. For an extended family filled with former music students, it was quite the achievement. As ever-proud parents humbled with each and every victory, we became hesitant to broadcast the news by the third and fourth wins. Not wanting to appear boastful or stir any green-eyed monsters, we chose to celebrate quietly though still brimming with pride.

As a further enticement to enrol and make it less of a financial nightmare for us, Camille was awarded the prestigious Lillian Disney Scholarship, named in honour of Walt Disney's wife. It provided more than half the tuition fees. Still, we worried. How would we cover the balance? "We'll manage somehow.... This is their chance.... They have to go," my husband reassured me when Camille wasn't around. The sacrifices parents are willing to make for their children. The reality of having our child leave home had not sunk in. They'd never been on their own before. How would they manage without us? And what would our lives be like without them? We knew other parents who were ready to move on to the next stage and elated to get their kids out the door. We were not those parents. Like the David Bowie song "Kooks," we strived to be a carefree, fun-loving family and enjoyed our time together as a happy trio.

Camille's love of music and art emerged at a young age, and their talents were quickly recognized by several teachers and even strangers, who urged lessons. These promptings reinforced what we already knew, but we refused to be those competitive parents, the type who militantly enforced practice or study time. There were so many other things to do, places to go, music to listen to, films to watch, art exhibits to see. We nurtured without nagging and Camille excelled. Our bright star had grown and moved away, leaving the band behind to play on.

When we arrived at the university, few parents were to be seen. We couldn't help but wonder, Were we being too overprotective, too involved? Were we robbing Camille of independence by being here? It'll be sink or swim soon enough, we reassured each other later. We had always shared a close bond with our only child and wanted the door of communication to remain open so they'd always feel they could turn to us if needed. But does any parent ever truly let go?

Wandering around campus amid pastel-coloured low-rise buildings, we marvelled at the palm trees, cacti, and wildflowers. The intense sun and rising heat scorched and exhausted us during our countless shopping trips. Languidly, we shuffled from store to store and then back again, relieved to return to the air-conditioned grad residences in Ahmanson Hall. Dripping with sweat, we trudged up and down stairs, dodging tiny geckos as they darted by, careful not to drop our awkward loads. Except for the electric rice cooker, which eluded us at every store, we'd found most of the essentials: jumbo packs of nori, a twenty-pound bag of brown rice, ready-to-eat pho noodles, a lidded wok, a teapot with infuser, and some donburi-style bowls — identical to ones we had back in Toronto, just in a different colour. The comforts of home to help settle in.

From an early age, Camille was clearly my husband's child. People recognized Gaëtan in their large blue eyes and dark wavy hair but did not see me in our striking child. I was often mistaken for the nanny. Back then the old questions of my youth resurfaced, this time from Camille's classmates: "Are you

Chinese? You have a Chinese head!" Over the years I've gone
through stages where I look more or less Asian or more or less
white. From years of experience, I've concluded you never know
how the genes are going to line up and change over time. In fact
I've never really looked like either of my parents. Looking in
the mirror these days, my hair has evolved from bone straight
to full-on curly. How did this happen?

Gaëtan always embraced his role as the fun guy and shared
a close bond with his only child, a miniature version of himself.
It was uncharacteristic for Camille to ignore his advice, yet now
in California resisted his repeated promptings to purchase a
tool kit. In this unfamiliar place they suddenly had the desire
to avoid all clutter. My husband is not one to argue. Just like
my grandfather, both men believed in fixing things and were
known to work tirelessly to get the job done. They understood
the utility of tools and owned their fair share of them; they
liked to work with their hands, to build something solid, something that would last. Neither had time for idle chit-chat.

I wanted to stay and help unpack, but the other activities
on the agenda didn't include parents. Before we knew it, we
were quickly ushered out of the place once we had completed
the basic move-in tasks. "They want to organize things on their
own. Let them do it their own way," Gaëtan admonished when
we were alone in the car.

Through heavy traffic the next morning, we inched our way
back to the airport. As we passed the looming LAX sign, it
caught our attention like unwitting, gawking tourists experiencing yet another milestone together. We texted Camille as
we waited for our flight. And once back at home and into our
daily routines, it was like we were all still together at any given
moment. There was some comfort in knowing we were only

a call or text away, unlike the generations before us who were left wondering and waiting for a letter with some news. Our daily check-ins with FaceTime kept the separation anxiety to a minimum.

Yet every time I passed that room on the second floor, I couldn't help but look in. I missed seeing my baby sitting in there. The space was now devoid of life but hardly empty. As it stood, I could barely get in the door. In the effort to pack for California, Camille had abandoned some things, strewn room by room, throughout the house. The battle to maintain an orderly home had been lost long ago. Where had I gone wrong? I wondered.

A new task presented itself: the slow and painstaking job of cleaning out a lifetime lived in one room. One weekend, a few weeks after our return from LA, we went in with vacuum, mop, and cleaning supplies at the ready. An enormous effort followed as we tried to re-create a sense of order where none seemed to exist. We excavated years of dust and cobwebs, rediscovered lost clothes in the piles of dirty laundry, and found a hoard of unused sketchbooks and art supplies, along with random drawings mixed in with forgotten music scores, all waiting to be sorted and filed. In Camille's absence, we reconnected with the fragments of a life left behind.

In one box I discovered a treasure trove of Japanese items: kid's books, school texts and workbooks, origami paper, and Hello Kitty and anime collectibles. I pulled out the woodblock featuring Camille's Japanese name written in kanji. Grandpa carved the Chinese character years ago. One weekend when he visited Auntie Aiko's cottage, she encouraged her dad to try out her new Dremel carving tool. Camille was thrilled when he presented it. I polished the block and placed it front and centre on the bookshelf — a welcome home reminder of where it all began.

"Who raised this slob?" I asked my husband as we sifted through the debris. We did our best to organize things for the anticipated return, ever hopeful these things would eventually get sorted out.

• • •

Is it possible we inherit traits?

When my grandparents moved from Browning Avenue to their condo, they found a huge cache of art supplies in Grandpa's study. "We would buy him really nice paper and he would use nothing but scraps," Mom recollected. He stockpiled the gifts he received over the years: fine silk and rice paper, *sumi-e* ink, oil paints, brushes, art boards, canvases. Many items remained unopened. Once he retired Grandpa attended some *sumi-e* lessons for older adults and spent hours practising his brush strokes on odd scraps of paper, used envelopes, or newspapers — from *sumi-e* basics such as bamboo trees and animals to writing Japanese words in a type of stylized calligraphy called *shodō*. "He was such a perfectionist," Mom said. "Your sister comes by it honestly."

Grandpa's kids urged him to do a good copy of something, anything. But in his mind, it never measured up. Much of what he did produce he destroyed. As a self-taught artist, he remained his harshest critic and rarely allowed himself the luxury of using real art supplies. Grandma wasn't sure if he was too proud and didn't want to show off or if he just didn't want others to see his work. "He never thought it was perfect enough. He threw them all out. When he died there was nothing. I have nothing that he did."

When they lived in prison camps during the war, Grandpa was one of about a half-dozen men who helped chop wood.

Everyone needed wood, but not every household had men since most of them had been sent away to forced labour camps. Grandma remembers two wood-burning stoves in their shack. "All kinds of logs were dumped off and Grandpa would bring home the wood. With that wood, the men made all sorts of things," she recalled. Occasionally, if he had any free time after finishing work in the mess hall, Grandpa carved vases from wood scraps. Some of them were given to relatives for use on their family altars. Mom has two of those vases. She remembers asking him for them a long time ago. "He always pooh-poohed his art, so he couldn't understand why I would want them. 'What do you want these things for?'" Mom mimicked Grandpa's stern questioning. "'Because you created them.'"

To him they were pieces of junk. One vase was fashioned from an actual root, which he had managed to expertly hollow out and polish to a fine sheen. The other resembled a block of wood with its corners smoothed over. On one side he painted a tiny scene of two swans, one black and one white, swimming among lily pads. Never filled with water, these vases sat in our living room when we lived down the street from Grandma's. When Mom left for Florida, she took these treasured items with her. They're still on display in her condo.

A framed watercolour hangs in a place of honour in my aunt Judy's dining room. With its painted green background, the small image is unmistakably of a black-and-white chicka-dee. Grandpa was upset when he saw it one holiday gathering. He never wanted to have his work displayed and asked, "Why did you do that? That one was no good." His daughter happened on it by accident during a visit one day. Grandpa used the adjoining sunroom behind their bedroom as his private study. Aunt Judy was upstairs looking for something to write

Sumi-e watercolour painting of fish by Shigeru Nakamura.

on and, shuffling through the junk pile of papers on his desk, something caught her eye. Finding the picture, she was amazed at how well done it was. Quietly, she showed it to Grandma before taking it home, without ever mentioning it to Grandpa. Once it was framed, she added it to her collection of beautiful art. If you look closely, you'll notice it's closely cropped around the image to distract from the newsprint flyer it's painted on. "He was extremely talented. He had a delicate touch, which made his work realistic," said Aunt Judy.

For many JCs, studying the arts was viewed as a pastime or hobby, not something to be considered seriously. Business and medicine were subjects to be studied, careers to be pursued. "The kids had to have something concrete, a legitimate career instead of playing around with music or art. Only people of means had the time to do these things. There was no time for frivolity. Working-class people like us had to work for a living. That was his way of thinking," Mom remembered. This type of pragmatic thinking influenced them all. Grandpa waited until much later in life, when he finally had some leisure time, to pursue these hobbies. He often hid away in the basement or his study. Was he working on something, or did he just want to get away from all the noise? Mom was never sure.

When Camille enrolled in university, family and friends asked, "What do they plan to do after studying music?"

"Get a job," we'd shrug. What else could we say?

Growing up, everyone took piano lessons, but few still know how to play, me included. Grandma remembers when the family moved into the house on Duchess Street, the previous tenants had left behind a broken-down organ that all the kids wanted to play. As a child, Mom enjoyed sitting at the push-pedals, plunking away even though a few of the keys didn't work. No one from the older generation had music training or owned a piano. But everyone knew how to sing and most knew how to dance, a throwback to regional life in Japan when the men and women celebrated after the harvest. Grandma recalls, "In those days, only rich people had a piano."

Despite this, Grandma wanted her kids to have music lessons. When the family moved to Browning Avenue, they replaced the old with new and bought an upright piano for about $300 — a big expense that no one questioned for a family of girls. And Grandma ensured all her children, even her son, received musical instruction, some with and some without Royal Conservatory of Music testing. Standing in the dining room and covered with portraits, the upright piano saw its share of players and acted as a family shrine.

And instead of being left behind, the aging organ was recast to play a more practical role. Grandpa saw potential in its quality craftsmanship. He reimagined it by removing the keyboard and inside mechanisms and converted it into an attractive and functional desk, which he kept in his study. Whether it was his creative streak or having lived through hardships during the war, true to the Japanese idea of *mottainai*, it went against his nature to be wasteful. Decades later, when my grandparents left for their condo, one of the aunts took the upright piano, but the old organ-turned-desk followed them and continued to be pressed into service.

When Grandma and Grandpa still lived in the house on Browning, we visited most Fridays. We made it our habit to drop by each week since we were just around the corner for baby Camille's weekly weigh-ins at the doctor's office on the Danforth. Grandpa loved to dote on his great-grandchild. Grandma scolded him when he joked around or acted silly, saying he never had time for his own kids. Whether in the dining room or the kitchen, Grandpa always sat at the head of the table. For each meal young Camille scrambled over and claimed a spot beside him, quickly growing taller each month.

Grandpa knew we weren't on easy street. What would he say now about grad school?

Were we being indulgent in allowing our child to study music and the arts? Would he think our good intentions were paving the way for few financial prospects in an uncertain future?

· · ·

Stepping out and starting a new life in uncharted territory was not a remarkable feat for a twenty-one-year-old. From Bāchan to Grandma to my mom — all these women were around the same age when they left their family homes. Like many young brides of their day, they were married to men they barely knew. Unlike Camille, their options were limited and pursuing advanced degrees unfathomable and elusive. Not to say they didn't believe in education; Bāchan was privileged to attend school, but it served little advantage once she arrived in Canada. Grandma fondly remembers attending a finishing course that taught sewing and cooking in Vancouver before her studies were cut short and she was needed at home. Mom says she didn't want to burden her parents with tuition fees — money they didn't have. When we were young children, she worked her way through night school. "Education is the way to move up in the world," Grandma often said.

Bāchan and Grandma made the best of their arranged marriages. They raised families, prospered, and appeared happy with the lives they had created for themselves. Both women became widows later in their lives and never dated or remarried. Family responsibilities took priority. My mother had the freedom to choose her own partner in marriage, but to a certain extent, her choices were still restricted. Because the JC community was forced to disperse and relocate after the war, there were few venues for JCs to meet one another. Marriage prospects within the culture were in short supply; the only Japanese men Mom knew, other than family, were a neighbour and a couple of classmates. Grandma's youngest sister, Masa, was the first to break with tradition and marry a Caucasian, Uncle Hugh, paving the way for the next generation. It couldn't have been easy for her, but it set a precedent and allowed my mom to be the first of her siblings to marry an outsider. "Are you sure this is what you want?" my grandparents asked Mom before welcoming my German father into the fold.

After centuries of Japanese unions, it was the beginning of intermarriage and a new evolution for our family. A decade later too many differing viewpoints pushed my parents apart. Despite being ambitious and hard-working like my mom, my father didn't know how to be a dad. His father had died during the war when he was young and his widowed mother had been forced to work. As a result he and his brother were sent to live with their grandparents in the German countryside. My father always told us his mother, our oma, had abandoned him and his brother as boys. He held this grudge against all women for most of his life.

We once visited Oma in Bremen, Germany. My sister, Dee, had a conference to attend and thought it presented an opportune excuse for a visit with our German relatives. Up for the adventure, Camille and I piggybacked on her trip with her daughter, Samantha. Keen to explore my father's hometown, with its rambling cobblestone streets and stunning UNESCO World Heritage site, we were fascinated by the multitude of museums and historical sites. And the kids delighted in discovering whimsical tributes around every corner to the Grimm Brothers' *Town Musicians of Bremen*. Oma's adopted daughter, Sabina, and her husband, Guntar, graciously picked us up from our hotel and chauffeured us to their large apartment for our family reunion. Oma greeted us, grinning ear to ear as happy tears streamed down her wrinkled face. Meeting her great-grandchildren for the first time, she embraced them with an unexpected strength for a frail-looking woman in her eighties.

In the spacious kitchen with built-in European appliances, Sabina, Dee, and Oma sat down at the small table. Sabina put away the apple strudel I bought from the bakery, and her daughter, Sarah, served the German tortes they made along with strong coffee for the adults. As the afternoon discussions wore on, Oma broke down, crying in anguish while recollecting how she had no choice but to work in the munitions factories during the war. At least she had some comfort knowing, despite all the hardships, her parents took good care of her sons. Only Dee knew enough German to understand what she was saying and filled in these details once we were back at the hotel. The rest us of stood around awkwardly in the smoke-filled room, occasionally pacing over to the open balcony door to breathe in some fresh air. We could see Oma was upset but had no words to share. Later we wondered if she had waited all this time to make this confession. A few months after we returned home, we received news she had died peacefully.

• • •

Early memories of my father are few. "Where's Dad?" I remember asking my mom. "Working," she always answered.

He left early in the morning and returned late at night; if we did see him, it was for only brief moments. One day he just disappeared, without fanfare or explanation. And throughout the years, he simply showed up for visits unannounced and when it suited him. My father liked to spend long days working, playing soccer, or staying out late drinking with his buddies, which was easier for him than being at home with his family. My mother wanted more for us and grew tired of the arrangement. She told us, "He became an embarrassment. Some nights he never came home. His behaviour was an insult, blatantly paraded in front of Grandma, Grandpa, and Bāchan. You kids didn't need to be exposed to that. So I told him to find somewhere else to live. As it was, he was hardly ever there and when he was, he didn't know how to interact with you kids." With a down payment borrowed from Grandma and Grandpa, Mom bought her own house and we moved down the street from my grandparents. During the early 1970s, Mom remained the only single parent in our large extended family, at our neighbourhood public school, and in the JC community. With the determination of Bāchan, she kept moving forward, leading by example, following her own path.

When my sister and I were much older, we asked my father what had gone wrong. "For starters," he told us, "I never liked rice."

• • •

My grandfather was a quiet man who personified what it meant to be a father. We knew we could always count on him and never once did he let us down. After Bāchan died Grandpa took her place as the permanent fixture at the Browning Avenue home.

When Camille was born, we asked him to suggest some Japanese names. Using hiragana or katakana, a name can be written phonetically in different ways, but it's usually the distinct kanji that provides the definitive meaning. Just about everyone in our family has more than one name. Some use their English name, while others prefer their Japanese one. While many are known by both, most of us don't know what the kanji for our name is — it was never written down. By providing a Japanese name in kanji, Grandpa helped set the tone, to define Camille's life and identity.

As a child Camille was known by both names, wavering back and forth between them depending on whether we were at Japanese school or in an English-speaking environment. By the time university days arrived, they had settled into using both names, proudly writing the kanji on all their original artwork and musical scores — a unique signature and distinguishing mark among artists.

CHAPTER 4

FIRST TO THE HORSE STALLS

STEPPING OUT OF a taxi at Victoria Harbour, the Nakamuras were swallowed into the horde of Japanese. Travelling from all over the lower island on short notice, the grim lot shuffled along the wharf beneath cloudy skies on that spring day in 1942. For the end of April, it remained mild and breezy as Yaeki Nakamura waded through the crowd, pushing baby Kathy in her cumbersome pram. Packed to the brim, it carried their allotted suitcase and a handful of oranges tucked in at the sides. Yaeki had just bought the ripe fruit. There was no way she was going to leave it behind to rot.

An Empress-style steam vessel had docked on the edge of the wharf. Arriving at the foot of the ship, Yaeki noticed a narrow gangplank on one side. Even though it had rope-style railings to hang on to, she wondered how to navigate the steep climb on her own when no one stepped forward to assist her. The large stroller wheels seemed too bulky to push up each step and the metal carriage was too heavy for her to lift. Her husband, Shigeru, had already gone ahead and boarded — busy helping his mother and younger siblings. Yaeki anxiously scanned each passing face, searching for someone familiar. Gradually, the snaking lines of people disappeared, swallowed whole into the ship's belly. Yaeki stopped for a moment to catch her breath. Gazing around and blinking in disbelief, she suddenly felt overcome with a wave of fear — she was the only person left on the pier.

Where is she? Shigeru must have been filled with worry, wondering what happened to Yaeki and the baby. Perhaps he ventured to the boat's edge and caught sight of her with the buggy on the dock below. Maybe someone had seen Yaeki and sent him out to fetch her. Embarrassed, he rushed back down the gangplank. Nervously, he grabbed the opposite side of the pram by its attached canopy with such force he broke the latch. The hood ripped open, sending the oranges flying. Mortified, the couple raced to snatch everything up before carrying the pram and baby to safety.

After Japan attacked Pearl Harbor on December 7, 1941, Canada acted swiftly and declared war against Japan. The War Measures Act, invoked at the start of the Second World War in 1939, had effectively branded thousands of people as enemy aliens, and now anyone of Japanese descent was considered suspect despite their status as Canadians. Fishing boats were confiscated and livelihoods suspended. Restrictions were imposed: JCs were excluded from British Columbia's hundred-mile security zone along the Pacific Coast; they needed to be ready to leave their homes within twenty-four hours' notice. Yet no one knew when the call would come or what would happen next. Curfew demanded lights out after dark and residents to remain inside. This meant no going out, not even for a walk.

Sun Cleaners immediately noticed a drop in business. Regular customers stopped frequenting the dry cleaners owned by Shigeru and Yaeki, located on Fort Street near Cook, where they both worked. They had moved to Victoria a year before and now wondered how they'd make ends meet. So many people were depending on them. The rented storefront had a two-bedroom flat behind the shop, where the couple lived with their new baby, Kathy; Shigeru's mother, Taki; and five of his siblings.

The escalation of targeted measures had everyone in the Japanese community on edge. The Nakamuras were forced to surrender their Cooey single-shot rifle to the British Columbia Provincial Police in October 1940. By February 1942 their radio and camera were confiscated. Their Plymouth coach, seized in early March, technically belonged to the bank since monthly car payments were still being made. While custodian files indicate a Chinese man wanted to purchase the vehicle for $650, Grandma recalled transferring ownership to a woman from the local jewelry store who offered to continue making the payments.

Shigeru approached the Willows Fairgrounds, where the Victoria exhibition was held, to ask if some of the family's belongings could be stored there indefinitely. The custodian agreed, and other Japanese followed Grandpa's lead. Before the end of April 1942, the order for relocation came. At the last minute, Shigeru found a buyer for Sun Cleaners and sold it for $500 to a Chinese family looking to buy at bargain-basement prices. Back at the flat, Yaeki rushed to pack her one suitcase: the young mother thought of her eight-month-old child's needs before her own, and baby Kathy's clothes and bulky diapers easily filled one bag. The rest was left behind.

On the back of this photo, in her distinctive cursive, Grandma has written, "Your loving sis, Yaeki. Taken on Dec. 16, 1941."

Though facing an uncertain future, the family were grateful to be together. Shigeru had been permitted to stay with his family, possibly due in part to having a young wife, a baby, and a widowed mother with many young children to care for. Most able-bodied men had already been taken away to forced work camps. "Over in Strawberry Hill, they came at midnight to pick the men up. My dad had no choice but to go," Grandma remembers. Any men who challenged the authorities, were caught outside during curfew, or committed misdemeanours were considered enemy prisoners of war (POWs) and sent to a remote barbed-wire enclosed camp:

> Male *Nikkei*, (471 *Nisei* and 295 *Issei*) aged 17 to 60 were held captive in a remote PoW camp at Angler in northern Ontario. They were composed of the "Nisei Mass Evacuation Group," a group who vowed they would evacuate only with the family intact, "security risks," "troublemakers," die hard Issei convinced of Japan's victory and young Nisei who followed their father, older brother or friends. Since they were confined as prisoners of war, they were guarded by the Army.... None of the more than 700 interned men were guilty of disloyalty and none were deported.[1]

Incarceration survivor Toyo Takata describes the setting in *Nikkei Legacy*: "Like the German PoWs in a separate compound at Petawawa, they followed the daily procedures of muster and roll call, and they wore a large red circle on their backs to provide ready target in any escape attempt. Any infraction of rules resulted in disciplinary action."[2]

Setting sail from Victoria, the ship ferried the Nakamuras and the last dispatch of Japanese people to the mainland. Unbeknownst to those aboard, in the wake of the historic moment, their former lives were washed away. The ship docked in Vancouver. Buses waited to drive the solemn group to their temporary home in the expansive Pacific National Exhibition (PNE) grounds located in Hastings Park. On arrival the detainees were divided before being shunted off to different accommodations: the women and children, including Yaeki, Taki, and the girls, were corralled into the Livestock Building; Shigeru and his brother Gord were sent with the other men to the Forum; and their youngest brother, George, like all boys aged thirteen to eighteen, was ushered to the dormitory for boys.

Built in 1929, the concrete-and-steel Livestock Building had been quickly converted into a large room filled with multiple army-issue bunk beds. Expanded to 142,000 square feet in 1939, the massive art moderne structure had a long history of housing livestock.[3] The straw and manure may have been cleared away, but the stench remained to welcome the new lot. Entering the building, the Nakamuras noticed most of the spots were already taken, marked by overhanging sheets and coarse blankets to enclose the claimed bunks for privacy. Some women had been held there for more than a month. Eventually, the group found an unoccupied spot with two bunk beds. Each bed had a thin and scratchy straw mattress, which provided little comfort for the uneasy travellers. Yaeki and baby Kathy took the bottom of one; Taki and her youngest daughter, Haru, took the other; and Taki's older daughters, Maki and Tomi, hopped up to claim the top bunks.

Family members were permitted to see one another during the day on the PNE grounds. Despite being housed in the same vicinity, they remained apart, and even the communal mess hall, located in a separate building, segregated the community. Men and boys ate on one side; women and children, on the other. The unfamiliar food and unsanitary conditions pushed the detainees to hold a one-day food strike, with hopes of returning to their diet of fish and rice. In *Nikkei Legacy*, Toyo Takata elaborates on the conditions:

> Women and children were assigned to the livestock building, which had not been properly cleaned or made sanitary. Dried manure was scraped off to make the quarters more habitable, but the distasteful smell lingered. Ventilation was inadequate and thick dust floated in the stale air. Privacy was nonexistent until they improvised with sheets and curtains; the latrines (not flush toilets) lacked partitions until they protested. Food was unappetizing, there was little fresh produce, a bland gruel was served for breakfast, and there were outbreaks of diarrhea to add to their misery. A food strike in protest had little effect. For the elderly, it was a long haul to the mess-hall, particularly in the rain.
>
> Some White staff within the compound exploited the situation. Gambling was prohibited but big-stake games continued openly with a member of the supervisory staff collecting a rake-off. For those willing

> to pay to supplement their lacklustre diet,
> an underground Japanese eatery operated
> within, with the covert sanction of an of-
> ficial, since supplies had to pass inspection
> at the gate and coal for cooking had to be
> diverted from the furnace bin. A guard or
> two attempted to take physical liberties with
> the women.[4]

Seventy years later these miserable living conditions were finally acknowledged. Many of the buildings, like the mess hall, are no longer standing. The Livestock Building, initially considered for demolition in 2010, received heritage designation to recognize its architecture and history. On December 1, 2012, on the grounds of the PNE in Hastings Park, the Vancouver Heritage Foundation unveiled a commemorative plaque outside of the building. The inscription reads as follows:

> **Livestock Building**
> Over 3,000 Japanese Canadian women, chil-
> dren and tuberculosis patients were unjustly
> detained here under traumatic and deplor-
> able conditions between March 1942 —
> March 1943. A public facility since 1929,
> the Livestock Building gained national his-
> toric significance as a federally authorized
> wartime marshalling site. The incarceration,
> confiscation of property, and forced dispersal
> from the coast of 22,000 innocent Japanese
> Canadians from 1942 to 1949 was officially

acknowledged as unjust by Canada in 1988.
In commemoration of all Japanese Canadians
Interned.

Gaman (Endurance) · *Giri* (Duty) · *Ganbare*
(Perseverance).[5]

By July 1942 the BC Security Commission announced families
would no longer be divided. They approved the return of married men forced into road camps, allowing them to rejoin their
families. But this only continued the effective removal of JCs
from the British Columbia coast. Some families, in an effort to
remain together, hastily agreed to work contracts on sugar beet
projects in southern Alberta and Manitoba.

Shortly after, the commission presented another option:
relocation to the remote mountain valleys of central British
Columbia. Hearing this news, Shigeru approached the authorities, asking to be reunited with his family. Before he knew it,
he and his brother Gord were en route to Popoff in Slocan with
a crew of men. In Slocan they spent long days building camp
housing and communal facilities. Located along the banks of
the Slocan River and surrounded by mountains in the remote
interior, the abandoned ghost town once thrived as a silver and
lead mining hub. The picturesque landscape soon became littered with rows of hastily built shiplap-and-tar-papered wood-
en shacks. Measuring about fourteen by twenty-eight feet, each
shack housed a minimum of six people. Families were expected
to lodge with whomever they were paired with.

By August 1942 the women and children exchanged one
enclosure for another. Leaving the Livestock Building behind,
they loaded onto trains set for the prison camps. Arriving in

Popoff, the Nakamuras piled into a cramped three-room shack. At least they didn't have to share with strangers. Shigeru, Yaeki, and baby Kathy claimed one bedroom, and the other bedroom housed Taki and five of her children (Maki, 22; Gord, 20; Tomi, 19; George, 15; and Haru, 13). That same month my mother, baby Kathy, celebrated her first birthday in town with the Goto family, but there was no cake or ice cream for the young prisoner.

Grandma remembers two wood-burning stoves in the centre room: a kitchen stove where they did the cooking and a pot-bellied camp stove used for heating. The makeshift kitchen also contained a dining table and a sink that emptied into the ground. Water had to be fetched from a tap about fifty yards away. The washroom, essentially a large room filled with many toilets, was located behind their shack and shared among several other families. To access this longhouse, you had to cross a shallow trench-like ditch via a makeshift bridge. For the young, old, and not-so-able-bodied, having to navigate this fear-inducing narrow plank of wood during the day provided enough of an ongoing trial, let alone the unease of making one's way at night or during the cold winter.

The communal baths were used by the entire village. Built like Japanese-style bathhouses, there were two separate structures: one for women and children and the other for men. Each tub fit about five people and the water was changed daily. Before soaking in the deep tub, or *ofuro*, you'd wash in another area with a basin, towel, and soap. Having all bathers washed and rinsed before entering the *ofuro* kept the water clean for as long as possible.

During the day Shigeru supervised the kitchen staff and helped the cooks in a large tent set up as Popoff's mess hall. A year of living day-to-day in uncertainty passed, and in the fall of 1943, Yaeki and Shigeru welcomed their second daughter, Irene, born in the Slocan City hospital.

Taki's two oldest daughters, Toshie and Kiyoko, were already married, and my great-aunts remained with their families in Black Mountain, near the isolated interior of Kelowna, British Columbia. Already living in a remote area far from the hundred-mile security zone, they weren't forced to relocate. Toshie, her husband, three children, and father-in-law lived and worked on the Kelly orchard and farm as sharecroppers. Kiyoko's family were living in North Vancouver when they received the evacuation notice. Kiyoko immediately contacted Toshie and arranged to join her family. Within days the couple and their young son boarded the train for Kelowna.

During the fall harvest season, many young people worked as labourers. Before the first summer was over, my great-uncle Gord left Popoff for an orchard in Vernon and remained there, picking fruit and pruning trees, until 1945. Whenever he had the chance, he'd visit his sisters and their growing families in the nearby Kelowna area. Back at the camp, my great-aunt Maki started a job as a nurse's aide at the new hospital in Slocan City, working night shifts and sleeping during the day. There she met her future husband, a young medical student named Kiichi.

Thinking they'd be able to return home once the war ended, many Japanese had simply locked up their possessions in their houses or farms. They didn't know they'd never see their things again. Everything they owned was taken and auctioned off without their knowledge or consent. Some of the proceeds were used to pay for their incarceration costs. The Nakamuras were of modest means and only rented the building where their dry cleaning business operated. Unable to store any items there once their business was sold, they left their belongings at the Victoria Willows Fairgrounds. But as the summer exhibition approached, the short supply of storage space led to a clearing, and fortunately for the Nakamuras, their items were shipped to Slocan. As meagre as a few pieces of furniture, some rice, and Yaeki's sewing machine were, the family considered themselves lucky to receive these items.

• • •

In the late 1920s the extended Goto clan proudly owned a combined farmstead of twenty acres along Gibson Road in Delta, British Columbia. Coincidently, on the south side of the road not far from their property, the Nakamura family had built a log cabin before leaving the area for Salt Spring Island. Though not acquainted as neighbours, the two families eventually met years later and became closely intertwined.

Unlike the Nakamuras, my grandmother's side of the family had been torn apart. In the former Strawberry Hill area, her mother and siblings did their best to manage the farm on their own. Most of the men, including Grandma's father, Yasukichi Goto, were rounded up months earlier and taken away to work camps. Yasukichi's wife, Miyoshi, like the other Japanese women with families who were left behind, worried about being separated from her children when called to evacuate. The only option was to agree to work on a sugar beet farm. In June 1942 she and her five children (Nellie, 17; Tin, 15; Tomo, 13; Sakae, 11; and Masa, 8) packed what personal belongings they could carry and took the long train ride to Alberta. Everything else remained behind at their five-acre farm. A few years later nothing was spared — every item was appropriated and auctioned off without their knowledge by the Office of the Custodian of Enemy Property. In *Who Was Who: Pioneer Japanese Families in Delta and Surrey*, Michael S. Hoshiko indicates, for all their hard work and suffering, the Gotos received a cheque for $587.[6]

The train carrying Miyoshi and her children stopped in Calgary to pick up more families before heading to Lethbridge. On arrival the Gotos waited patiently to meet their new employer. When no farmer claimed them and four other families, they were all escorted by RCMP officers back to the train station for the journey to Nelson, British Columbia. From there they were bused to the interior relocation centre in Slocan City:

> With a sinking feeling of uneasiness, the tired travellers stepped off the coach to face the curious onlookers and the assembled farmers, with their trucks and horse-drawn hay wagons, waiting to claim their chosen families. It was a picture of ironic contrasts as the apprehensive refugees, decked in their Sunday best, were stonily greeted by their new masters in work clothes. By roll call, the family and their farmer-employer were matched up. It did not always work out as some families had difficulty in being placed; some farmers reneged on the pre-selection arrangement, being dissatisfied with the "lot" assigned to them.[7]

Though my grandmother's mother and siblings were spared from the Hastings Park experience, in this twist of events,

Goto family postcard, Slocan, 1943. From left: Masa, Sakae, Nellie, Miyoshi, Tomo, and Tin.

they managed to end up nearby in the Slocan City incarceration camp. Located about a twenty-minute walk from the Nakamuras' shack in Popoff, the Goto family lived in the town. Miyoshi's nickname, Tanabāchan, was coined from "Town-no-bāchan," which combined the English word "town" with the Japanese word for "grandma." Once relocated to Slocan City, Miyoshi remained separated from her husband, Yasukichi.

My great-grandfather Yasukichi arrived in Canada in 1920 and joined his brother Bunji, who had settled on River Road in the town of Sundry, in Delta. Earlier that year, back in their hometown of Miyagi-ken, Japan, a twenty-two-year-old Yasukichi married Miyoshi Sato, but when she became pregnant, he decided to journey alone. Wanting to establish himself before he sent for her, a few years passed before he met his first child, Yaeki. In December 1923, with fifty dollars and her nearly three-year-old child in tow, Miyoshi boarded the *Alabama Maru* steamer in Japan. After two weeks in third-class passage, the mother and child arrived in Canada.

Yasukichi worked in logging camps and timber mills. While acting as a millwright in a sawmill, the young father suffered a near-fatal head injury when a large tree fell the wrong way. He switched to farming and by 1929 had saved enough to purchase a farm plot near his brother at 1327 Gibson Road. They raised chickens and grew mainly strawberries as a member of the Strawberry Growers' Nokai, but they also grew currants and gooseberries. Yasukichi's advanced carpentry skills were often in demand, and he helped to construct many homes and chicken houses on Kennedy Road and in the surrounding Surrey area.

Eventually, farms gave way to development, which removed the homesteads and eradicated the countryside where so many Japanese once lived and toiled. Most physical markers have been erased, swept away by time. Few remnants of these early pioneers remain as the landscape changed from rural to urban. You won't find Gibson Road on any current map. I was able to track it down in old city council reports. That name exists only as a memory, and it is now known as 90 Avenue, North Delta. One of the only reminders is the Gibson Elementary School, which sits on the road where farmers' fields once were. There's another public school with a small park at one end — both share the Strawberry Hill name and are considered part of Surrey, which borders Delta. The Sunbury area still exists too, but is considered a small neighbourhood located in North Delta and is just one of a few communities that make up Delta.

Yasukichi never fully recovered from his head injury. His faculties wavered as the years passed and he grew increasingly forgetful. His children Yaeki and Tin remember cruel classmates and unsympathetic neighbours who, rather than believe he had been injured in an accident, preferred to call their father foolish or feeble-minded. Much later, a huge telltale scar emerged as Yasukichi's hairline slowly receded. When that fateful late-night roundup took place in February 1942, the men from the area, including brother-in-law Yasuji and cousin Teruo, were marshalled off to Red Pass, British Columbia. Despite the Goto family's protests regarding his cognitive impairment, Yasukichi did not escape that midnight call.

One cold and snowy day, he quietly wandered off. What was he thinking? No one knows for sure. With all the talk of relocation, he may have worried about his family and felt the need to rush home. Perhaps he was tired of being held at the camp and wanted to free himself from the poor working conditions or remote site. Whatever his reasons and despite the extreme weather, Yasukichi was determined to get away. Found with severe frostbite, the forty-four-year-old was deemed a "security threat" by RCMP officers and escorted to Vancouver General Hospital. A friend spotted him with the officers and sent word to the family. Multiple efforts to have him released were to no avail. The family remained without their father.

Once Yasukichi recovered, the hospital transferred him to Essondale[8] in Coquitlam, British Columbia, on April 28, 1942. Uncle Tin remembers: "During our many visits before our own evacuation, we noted that my father seemed to accept the unfamiliar surrounding he was placed in and seemed to be quite content. In later years, when he could have been discharged, no amount of coaxing could make him leave. As his doctor told us, 'This is his home and haven; leave him here.'"[9]

. . .

In April 1945 the Department of Labour issued an ultimatum to all JCs — move east of the Rockies or repatriate to Japan:

> Everyone 16 and over in the BC relocation camps was required to appear before the RCMP to declare for Canada or for Japan. It was the hour of desperate decision: east over the mountains, or west across the ocean? The drive to prod them out stirred a hornets' nest of frenzy and confusion. The choice was not simple. It divided families. To remain meant hasty plans to reestablish themselves in an unfamiliar setting, a difficult problem for those with young children. If they could not be resettled directly, they would go to a hostel, a mini-version of Hastings Park in unheard-of places like Transcona, Manitoba; Neys or Fingal, Ontario; and Farnham, Quebec; to await yet another move.[10]

Money was scarce and decent jobs remained hard to come by. Legal restrictions limiting their movements had finally been lifted. The Nakamuras remained in the Popoff camp until June before making their life-changing decision. An exodus to Toronto began. Shigeru's sister Tomi left first, after she and a friend found jobs. Hospital staffer Kiichi also relocated but was not able to continue his medical studies since incarceration derailed those plans. He rented a place in the Fashion District along Spadina Avenue and managed to find work in a broom factory. Shigeru's sister Maki followed Kiichi, working as a domestic and then in a dress factory. They married in the fall of 1945 and later had two children.

In *Many Petals of the Lotus*, Janet McLellan describes the atmosphere awaiting them in Ontario:

> Toronto was hostile to Japanese Canadians both during and after the war. During the war years few individuals of Japanese heritage were allowed to reside in the city. Exceptions were mostly students and domestics.... Japanese Canadians continued to be subject to discriminatory treatment in Toronto, such as being refused service in restaurants or denied accommodation and employment. Many found employment with a Jewish firm or individual.[11]

The remaining members of the Nakamura clan endured the week-long train ride to Ontario, sitting and sleeping on hard wooden benches. Arriving in Chatham, they were met by their employer — a family they had known on Salt Spring Island — and taken to a farm in Charing Cross. In these rural outskirts, the Crackle family grew tobacco, sugar beets, and tomatoes. Work paid twenty-five cents per hour and included accommodation, which the growing family needed. Shigeru and Yaeki welcomed daughter Aiko that winter.

Uncle Tin in Slocan, 1943.

Initially, the Goto family considered moving to Japan, but two weeks before the deadline, Miyoshi changed her mind. Her only son, Tin, found farm work in Ontario near the Nakamura clan. He had grown up fast, without his father, and assumed responsibility for the family early on. Two years of hard farm labour ensued for both families, but they were happy to be in close proximity again. In 1947 Shigeru got a call from his sister Maki in Toronto: a presser was needed right away at the dress factory where she worked. Shigeru wasted no time and jumped on the offer. Then and there, on hearing the news their older brother planned to leave, all the other men decided if *niisan* is going, we are too.

Both Nakamura and Goto families packed their bags and headed for Toronto in February 1947. With everyone pooling their money, they raised $4,000 and purchased a former boarding house on Duchess Street, which is now known as Richmond Street East. Described as Grand Central Station, the home, known to the family as simply "Duchess Street," provided a secure foothold and ready springboard for two close-knit families. The downtown location provided easy access to St. Lawrence Market. Grandma remembers surprising the fishmonger when she asked for a large fish with the head on. Most people wanted small deboned filets. She explained she had a big family before walking home with the fresh fish. Urban development began to change the area, and it wasn't long before the fish heads were no longer free.

The Nakamura family continued to grow. Three more daughters were born (Yuki, Judy, and Marlene). Most of Shigeru's siblings married and moved out to start families of their own. The Gotos found a home in the East York area, where Miyoshi and her five children (Nellie, Tin, Tomo, Sakae, and Masa) settled.

In April 1949 JCs were finally granted voting rights.

Shigeru's sister Tomi married that same year and moved to Fort William, now called Thunder Bay, where her husband's business was located. Her husband succumbed to cancer in 1955, and she returned to Toronto with her two daughters to be closer to family. Brother Gord married in 1951, and youngest sister Haru married a year later, in 1952.

By the time the Nakamura family moved to Browning Avenue in 1955, they were ready to usher in a new era of stability. The last of their eight children (Norma and Doug) were born. They returned to the dry cleaning business in 1956 when Shigeru and his sister Tomi started Mercury Cleaners with two locations: one on Gerrard Street, which Shigeru and Yaeki ran with some help from their kids, and the other on Queen Street East, where Tomi worked. George remained a bachelor and set himself up in the flat above the shop on Gerrard Street until 1961 when he finally married. Toshie, who still lived near Kelowna, took her first flight to attend George and Terry's wedding. The happy reunion with family convinced her and her husband to settle in Toronto. They, too, took a turn living above the cleaners after George vacated.

A new chapter had begun, a time for each family member to put down roots and raise the next generation. Strong bonds continued to be forged between family members. When times were tough, they knew they could count on one another. And with every achievement and success, they were there to celebrate. Ongoing challenges aside, they adapted to their changing environment, and many felt the worst was behind them. Together they shared a genuine desire to move ahead and better their circumstances. Through the individual contributions and efforts of these and other hard-working families, the JC community grew and expanded. Within a few decades the Nakamura clan swelled to about one hundred. At last count in 2019, it had ballooned to 213 and continues to grow.

• • •

My mother, Kathy, was the first of her siblings to venture to the West Coast after the war. She and my father decided to visit her grandfather Yasukichi Goto in September 1963. Short of funds, the thrifty young couple had just married and decided to spend their honeymoon driving to British Columbia. They bought a used convertible and later sold it for airfare when it was time to return to Toronto. While in Vancouver my parents visited some of the Goto family members who had returned to the area after the war. Mom had never met cousin Teruo or his family before, but his daughter Lillian kindly offered to show the newlyweds around during their stay and took them to Essondale Hospital.

Yasukichi sat outside on the vast grounds, enjoying the mild autumn day. Mom recalls, "I don't remember much except it was very strange — he took to your father right away and began speaking to him, all in Japanese. Of course, we didn't understand. Your father pretended to follow whatever Grandpa was saying. I remember Lillian remarking later that Grandpa didn't usually respond to complete strangers, even though it was explained to him who I was."

Although Yasukichi remained seated during the entire time they were there, he gave the appearance of being rather short in stature. Perhaps this could be attributed to his round, bald head. Mom wasn't sure. And while he seemed comfortable with them, she wondered if he had forgotten how to speak English. He ignored my mother during their visit but became very animated speaking to my father. As they parted ways and said their goodbyes, no one knew this first meeting would be their last and only time together. After a lengthy stay in Essondale, Yasukichi died in 1967 at the age of sixty-nine. Only his remains were reunited with his family in Toronto. Miyoshi had died in 1961, and her ashes awaited his. They were buried together in Pine Hills Cemetery.

Before my parents left the Browning Avenue abode in Toronto, the family warned them about travelling to the West

Coast during the rainy season. Mom remembers only beautiful weather and not a drop of rain during their entire holiday. After visiting her grandfather, she wanted to see her former lodgings and took the ferry to Victoria to search for the old Sun Cleaners shop. In its place the couple found a new sign hanging at 1054 Fort Street: "Browning Guns." Taken aback at the sight of it, Kathy thought, *What a strange coincidence.*

CHAPTER 5

THE CHURCH
BUDDHISTS BUILT

NEAR THE INTERSECTION of Cecil Street and Huron, a stone's throw from Toronto's main Chinatown along Spadina Avenue, a three-storey Victorian semi sits cloaked in neglect, a shadow of its former self. The flaking painted-brick facade at 134 Huron Street sports a smattering of graffiti, which is mirrored on the low wooden fence standing guard at the sidewalk. Recycling bins and an assortment of garbage have taken root where a tall maple tree once stood. And languishing in the middle of the yard, an old green sofa devoid of its cushions greets passersby with an air of resignation.

Back in the late 1940s, the abode sported divided pane glass windows and decorative trim on the base of the second-storey bay window. As you approached the covered porch, past the chain-link gate and tidy fenced enclosure, nothing suggested you were entering a place of worship. Terry Watada's *Bukkyo Tozen*[1] details how the property, purchased by the Toronto Young Buddhist Society (TYBS) in 1947, served several functions for Toronto's first Buddhist organization. Religious services were held on the main floor, and members were permitted to use the kitchen on the second floor. It was part of the shared domain of Rev. Takashi Kenryu Tsuji and his wife, Sakaye, who called the two upper floors home following their incarceration in Slocan. Unlike the Buddhist priests who travelled from Japan to preside over temples in Canada, Tsuji, a second-generation JC, was the first nisei priest to oversee this new central hub and its activities. In May 1968 he became the first nisei bishop at Buddhist Churches of America (BCA).

Though some of the mainstream knowledge of Buddhism can be credited to the Dalai Lama and celebrities who practise the faith, the last century of its history in Canada is directly related to the JC community. Their dedicated efforts paved the way for other branches and contributed enormously to the development of Buddhism in Canada:

> The story of Buddhism in Canada is told in two parts: before and after 1967. Before 1967, the scene of Buddhism in Canada is painted chiefly with the Japanese in the foreground. It was the Japanese who built the first Buddhist temple in Vancouver in 1905, and it was also the Japanese Jodo Shinshu Buddhists who built the first Buddhist churches in the provinces east of British Columbia, in Alberta at the end of the 1920s, Toronto in the 1940s,

Manitoba in the 1950s, and Quebec in the
1960s. Their story is a tale of struggle against
overt and systematic discrimination marked
by such incidents as the Anti-Asiatic Riot of
1907 and the forced removal of the Japanese
into relocation camps during the Second
World War.[2]

Despite what the word "church" suggests with its Christian
undertones, the Toronto Buddhist Church (TBC) is dedicated
to the worship and education of Jodo Shinshu Buddhism, or
Shin Buddhism, as founded by Shinran Shonin (1173–1262)
in Japan. When the TBC first organized, it was affiliated
with a larger organization, the BCA,[3] which is a part of Nishi
Hongwanji, the mother temple and international headquarters
in Kyoto, Japan. While the TBC still shares ties to Japan, they
are now part of Jodo Shinshu Buddhist Temples of Canada.[4]
Formerly known as Buddhist Churches of Canada (BCC),
it started as Canada Kaikyo Kantoku Ku in the early 1930s.
During the Second World War operations disbanded but were
replaced in 1946 by the Buddhist Foundation of Canada (BFC),
which became part of the BCA. However in 1967 the BFC suspended activities at which time the BCC revived itself as an
independent and became a separate district with its own bishop
in 1968.[5] It is the largest foreign-owned minority church group
in the JC community. Japanese immigrants were predominantly
Buddhist, so it was no surprise they formed or joined a Buddhist
organization once they settled in Canada.[6]

Without an existing community or supports, these early
Buddhists found life in Canada difficult: "The history and experience of Japanese Canadian Buddhists is unique. Excepting

First Nations people, no other religious and ethnic minority in Canada has suffered as much legal discrimination and racism. The relocation and internment of more than twenty-three thousand Japanese Canadians in British Columbia, and their forced resettlement in eastern Canada following the Second World War, destroyed long-established community bonds and networks."[7]

By the 1950s the growing Japanese Canadian Buddhist community and lack of privacy for the Tsujis at 134 Huron Street led to a search for a new home. Incorporated in July 1952, the organization continued these efforts, with the goal of finding a permanent hall. Neighbourhood complaints about the increasing number of Japanese people using the premises led to a prohibition on holding meetings from Toronto City Hall. By 1955 the organization found a wonderful spot in Toronto's nearby Annex neighbourhood at 918 Bathurst Street. The modern temple known as the TBC was built just north of Bloor and a short walk from the Bathurst subway station. Fifty years later, concerns about the aging building structure and absence of ample street parking on Bathurst Street precipitated a move to North York. The perfect lot presented itself at 1011 Sheppard Avenue West. Located steps from the Downsview (now called Sheppard West) subway station, it provided an opportunity to build a much larger temple.

While working at Japanese Social Services (JSS) in the early 2000s, I met Tom Allen, a JSS board member, devout Buddhist, and former TBC president. He shared his early introduction to the TBC when I asked how he became affiliated with the temple. Raised a Christian, Allen planned to marry a JC woman named Hisaye. When he approached his church to make wedding arrangements, the young man was taken aback when his minister advised him to reconsider his choice and find a nice white girl to marry. Disappointed by this lack of inclusion, he questioned his faith. Hisaye's family provided a sharp contrast to this. The Buddhists welcomed him and shared his basic tenets of goodwill and tolerance. Allen converted and became involved in the community.

Allen explained there was no specific designation to register a Buddhist temple when the organization was founded. Rather than create a stir, the members accepted the city's administrative shortcomings and swapped out "temple" for "church" to create their memorable name. Amy Wakisaka, TBC's director of the Living Dharma Centre, says it was a conscious decision in both Canada and the U.S. as a way of assimilating and minimizing the discrimination and racism during those early years.[8] Janet McLellan elaborates: "Being a despised religious and racial minority, and reacting to the background of historical discrimination, community dislocation, and family disruption, Japanese-Canadian Buddhists made active attempts to accommodate their Jodo Shinshu beliefs and practices to Christian forms and to push their children into rapid assimilation."[9]

In the early 1990s younger members started questioning the earlier period of Christian assimilation and began to reintroduce Buddhist terms such as "temple" for "church" and "dharma talk" for "sermon." In 2008 the umbrella organization, BCC, felt the prejudiced threats of the past no longer existed and it was safe to change its name to Jodo Shinshu Buddhist Temples of Canada. The TBC, however, had already incorporated its name and built the new temple; going through the additional effort and expense seemed impractical.

• • •

While most of my family is Christian, my grandmother's side of the family is Buddhist. For as long as I can remember, we've celebrated Christmas Eve with our Buddhist relatives, complete with sushi platters, Christmas carols, and Santa and his helpers. Like many JC families, we share this duality of traditions and cultures with acceptance — even if neither side fully knows or understands the ins and outs of either faith.

Bāchan and Grandma converted to Christianity after moving to Canada, yet they both maintained an altar of sorts, or *kamidana*, which displays photos of deceased relatives. On certain holidays offerings were added: a flower arrangement, *gohan* (cooked rice) on a small footed dish, or a thimble-sized sip of sake. When I was old enough to notice these things and asked why, Grandma answered, "You can't change how we were raised." I've seen more elaborate *obutsudan*, or Buddhist shrines, with incense burners at my great-aunts' homes. I was tempted to buy one of the small architectural wonders at the temple, attracted by the beautiful black lacquer and intricate design. Instead, I have my own spot in the living room where I keep photos of departed family members.

As kids we went to Sunday school at St. Barnabas on the Danforth. It was walking distance from our house and comprised a mostly white congregation, but it had a Japanese connection. The minister, Rev. Vincent Goring, had lived in Japan before settling into the neighbourhood with his family of five children. Mom's younger sisters and brother knew some of the kids from school. I remember the stately Anglican church filled with stained glass windows, rows of wooden pews, an ornate carved altar, and a large commanding organ with soaring pipes. The children were ushered in from the basement for the opening hymns but then whisked out before the sermon began.

We'd go out through a side door and return downstairs so as not to disturb the sober procession.

At some point we joined St. Andrew's Japanese Congregation at St. Alban-the-Martyr Anglican Church on Howland Avenue. Deemed of historical and architectural interest by the Ontario Heritage Trust in 1992, the church received wide recognition for its grand style, soaring ceilings, intricate woodwork, and stained glass works of art. We shared the imposing neo-Gothic cathedral with the church's own parish and their main tenant, the Royal St. George's College, an independent school for boys.

Over the years our group of JCs shrank and we needed to find a new location. The private school continued to expand and eventually outgrew its existing rental space. It decided to build new facilities around the church and pressed to purchase the land for its exclusive use. The remaining parishioners from St. Alban-the-Martyr tried to fight the sale from going through, fearing the worst would happen once they were no longer there as advocates.[10] For all the local opposition, the school eventually purchased the entire grounds and church in 2000. The property has since been completely overhauled but, true to the school's word, the historic church remains.

Many of us felt a sentimental attachment to the old church; it was the site of baptisms, confirmations, family weddings, annual bazaars, and community events. We were reluctant to leave in the spring of 1994, but there was nothing we could do. Instead, the small group of faithful constituents from St. Andrew's Japanese Congregation relocated to St. David's Anglican Church on Donlands Avenue, mere steps from the Danforth, in time to celebrate Easter Sunday. Tiny by comparison and modest with its pretty hand-stencilled interior, the new location provided a welcoming sanctuary.

My sister, Dee, approached the minister, Rev. Sonjie Pearson, and asked for special permission to use St. Alban-the-Martyr one last time. Dee was married in the grand old church on Thanksgiving weekend, resplendent in the white silk kimono Grandma made with help from Auntie Kay. The fine autumn day and warm sunshine were perfect for taking photos — we stood outside, without our jackets, among the fallen leaves in this fitting farewell.

St. Andrew's Japanese Congregation traces its roots back to 1944. After the war many JCs settled in Toronto, and a collection of Anglicans wanted to worship together in Japanese. They organized their first service in the diminutive St. George's Chapel, which seats about thirty people and is located within the massive St. James Cathedral. The *Anglican Journal*[11] details how the initial service, presided over by former bishop of mid-Japan Heber James Hamilton, had about a dozen people in attendance but slowly grew. Hamilton was a missionary who travelled to Japan in 1892 and became the first diocesan bishop in 1912, a post he held for twenty-two years. He resigned in 1934 and, already in his seventies, returned to live in Toronto until his death in 1954. Other Japanese-speaking ministers followed. Reverends Paul Ken Imai, Roland Kawano, Sonjie Pearson, Warren Wilson, and Joan Wilson were integral to the community — they helped us celebrate family births and mourn every death as stewards to our essential rites of passage.[12]

St. Andrew's Japanese Congregation celebrated their seventy-fifth anniversary after Thanksgiving in October 2019. A special service complete with cake cutting included mention of twenty-five years spent at St. David's. The current minister, Rev. Joan Wilson, paid tribute to those twelve founding members from St. George's Chapel, one of whom was still alive.

There was no anniversary celebration for Dee. Her marriage ended years before, but the beautiful wedding kimono had its own tribute. Both Grandma and Grandpa were longtime members of the Wynford Seniors' Club. The group met a couple of times a month for bowling and other social activities. In the mid-1990s, the club decided to put on a craft show to showcase their members' talent in the auditorium of the former JCCC. Grandma had a booth where she hung the kimono alongside some of her award-winning framed *bunka shishū*, which demonstrated her skill in Japanese embroidery. I remember visiting and admiring the professional-looking set-up. An older Japanese woman Grandma knew dropped by. Placing her hand behind a section of the painstakingly beaded material, she lifted it for a closer look and gasped as she admired the intricate beauty. Grandma stood beaming and bowing in thanks, proud to be recognized for her efforts and craftsmanship.

Auntie Kay helped Grandma with the kimono. Our great-aunt was married to Uncle Tin, Grandma's only brother. A talented cook and professional seamstress, the former sample sewer radiated all things Japanese with her quiet demeanour, dainty frame, white-powdered face, and long hair always worn in a classic bun. Once the material had been cut into kimono-style panels for the patterning, Grandma spent long hours hand stitching and slowly piecing the garment together. To highlight and embellish the rose pattern in certain areas of the fabric, the women took turns with the time-consuming and detailed hand-beading. An incredible labour of love — and a work of art.

It wasn't a traditional wedding kimono. Inspired by Japanese design, Dee envisioned a hybrid garment that reflected her heritage and made detailed sketches of a chrysanthemum-pattern material. Searches in Toronto did not yield any suitable fabric. During a visit to Mom in Florida, she found the material — not Japanese silk or one featuring *kiku*, but a heavy, rose-patterned silk jacquard. The obi was another interpretative gesture and matched the kimono by repeating the rose pattern in lace. Sewn as more of a stylized cummerbund in front, the back featured a chiffon bow flourish and detachable train. In following the "something borrowed" tradition, Auntie Kay lent Dee her stiff formal collar, a piece that's worn under the kimono.

When Bāchan was still alive, she had shown Grandma how to make a kimono pattern. Time and time again, Grandma put those skills to the test by sewing many a kimono for the family. Where any of those kimono are now, she cannot say. Some had been loaned out, and she wondered if they had ever been returned.

· · ·

Our visits to TBC were purpose driven: funerals, weddings, and the annual bazaar. The actual structure doesn't fit the standard image of a church or temple. Double doors of the A-frame building open into a lobby with two sets of stairs on one side, similar to a 1970s-style side split. An open staircase leads up to the *hondō*, or main hall of the temple.

As a small child of about six, I was curious to see what was upstairs. I didn't know what to expect. Peeking my head through the open doors, I was immediately struck with the sacredness of the space — a large, serene room filled with the smell of lingering incense. Strips of redwood lined the steep pitched ceiling, and the altar at the end was minimal in design.

Devoid of pews, there were stackable chairs, which were easily moved or added as needed. It was unlike any church I'd ever been in. The minister, wearing a full-length black robe, stepped out and startled me with his quiet "Hello." I bolted down the first set of stairs. Quickly glancing upward to the top of the landing, the slight Japanese man smiled back at me serenely as I dashed down the second flight to the basement.

Downstairs was the complete opposite. It featured a wide open space where kids ran around amongst the hubbub of activity. Outfitted as classrooms with blackboards, the smaller adjoining rooms used by the Dharma school contained kid-sized tables and chairs and a variety of English- and Japanese-style toys. At the back of the building, a stainless-steel kitchen bustled with heavy use at every gathering. During most visits I saw my cousins, great-aunts, and great-uncles on Grandma's side of the family busily working away in the background.

At the annual bazaar each fall, the venue became so packed, it was standing room only. Lineups to buy food tickets from the basement dining area often snaked down the hallway and upstairs to the main floor. During the lunchtime rush, you were lucky to find a seat among the wall-to-wall tables to enjoy a steaming bowl of udon or tempura dinner. Others navigated the narrow perimeter, where plates of prepared desserts and green tea were sold as grab and go.

Upstairs the temple hall was transformed into a marketplace. Every year, especially in good weather, the event grew in popularity to the point where you literally felt the crush within the throngs of shoppers. Vendor tables lined the walls, mirrored by an interior square, each selling something different. Knowing the Japanese food vendors sold out quickly, people made a beeline for those tables, lunging at the stacks of boxed makizushi, inarizushi, and chow mein. Bags of frozen mochi were quickly snapped up, along with vegetable staples like daikon and gobo wrapped in newspaper and jars of the best homemade takuwan in the city. The requisite dessert table catered to those seeking baked goods and featured Japanese sweets like karintō and manjū. Assorted booths sold plants, books, or Japanese arts and crafts. Everything else, including an assortment of unusual items you could find nowhere else, was relegated to the white elephant section.

Though we weren't members, it felt sad to leave the building and its decades full of memories in 2005, even if the TBC was moving of its own accord. If buildings have karma, then that Bathurst Street temple must have done many a good deed. Unlike so many older structures in Toronto, it survived the wrecking ball. Miraculously, it found new life after it was sold — reincarnated as it were into an arts-and-cultural sanctuary by people who continue to recognize its origins. From 2015 to 2019, the former temple hosted Toronto Creative Music Lab (TCML),[13] an annual eight-day workshop culminating in a performance. It was a fantastic opportunity for early career musicians, ensembles, and composers to work with peer mentors in an environment encouraging artistic growth, learning, community building, and professional development. Camille was one of the performers chosen for the 2018 edition and remembers the thrill of collaborating with more seasoned musicians.

Throughout the week, Camille shared how strange it felt to be back in the temple, a place of some of their earliest memories. Workshop members had the opportunity to volunteer in different areas, and Camille chose to help in the kitchen with meal prep. "It reminded me of the commercial kitchen in the new temple and how important food is in our community." Important or essential? Food, culture, and memories are inextricably woven into our psyche. I've often joked there would be a riot if any family gathering ran out of food.

On the final day of the June workshop, my husband and I attended the evening concert. Walking through those wooden doors at 918 Bathurst was like travelling through a porthole in time. With a skewed sense of nostalgia, everything verged on the edge of the familiar. Little, yet so much, had changed. Discovering the state-of-the-art recording studio at the top of the stairs behind the former temple hall set me off balance. The original *hondō* featured carpentry by my great-uncle and to see it preserved made us feel strangely at home in taking our seats, comforted to see the pitched ceiling remained intact and former altar repurposed into a stage. The group of forty artists, selected from around the world, debuted fifteen new works by different composers. Camille played guitar within a larger ensemble in two separate pieces: *BLOC* and *And Yet They Speak (Celebration)*.

Following four successful seasons, TCML performed their last show in 2019. Camille and I talked about what a loss it was for contemporary musicians. Time spent with the group had been enriching, and several issues became apparent and were reinforced. For example, Camille discovered both a scarcity and invisibility of JCs within the contemporary music scene. From Camille's perspective, most Torontonians "don't know JCs exist, let alone the historical context" of the relocation after the war and how JCs became resettled and created the temple: "Only our trauma is amplified. Only internment is ever talked about without mentioning these people."

In many ways this reality is reflected in the larger community. Despite Japanese planting roots in Canada more than a hundred years ago, JC history is slowly being erased. Each generation adds their own perspective on identity and culture. Camille's generation — the gosei, or fifth generation — are almost entirely biracial. To the untrained eye, kids like Camille or their cousin Samantha easily pass for white. Just as my sister and I loosely resemble our parents, there are glimpses of us within our kids too. Our ethnicity may appear ambiguous, yet we share a rich cultural inheritance.

Canada's only Japantown in Vancouver is long gone. But here, in places like Markham's J-Town and the downtown Toronto strip called Little Tokyo, a string of savvy entrepreneurs have stepped in to serve up Japanese-infused shopping experiences. Do consumers ever ponder the roots of our community as they stand in line with their matcha lattes and mochi ice cream, hoping to get their pork belly ramen or stamped cheesecake before they sell out? Unlike these stores, which offer the latest trends and tastes of modern-day Japan, other long-established cultural and religious institutions scattered throughout the Greater Toronto Area reflect the perseverance of JCs who were determined to rebuild their lives after the war.

Will anyone remember their struggles or history decades from now? With so few Japanese in Canada, will anyone care? When searching for information, I discovered a dark void, a dearth of evidence, and little mention of our Japanese congregation or the people who dedicated their lives to it. A lost legacy in a disappearing community.

• • •

Swimming Upstream: Japanese Canadian Struggle for Justice in BC,[14] a film by community advisor and judge Maryka Omatsu, succinctly addresses the British Columbia government's role in three key areas: ethnic cleansing, property dispossession, and community destruction. This poignant documentary, narrated by JC author Mark Sakamoto, reveals how the government participated in actions leading to the shattering of our community despite assurances from the army, RCMP, and federal government that JCs posed no threat to national security. British Columbia made an official apology to JCs in 2012 but did it without the inclusion or knowledge of many community groups. It was "issued without prior community-wide participation. It did not formally assume responsibility for past injustices and was not followed by redress or legacy initiatives at the time, which many saw as a missed opportunity for meaningful follow-up and healing."[15]

In the spring of 2019, the National Association of Japanese Canadians (NAJC) began community consultations called BC Redress.[16] It reached out to local JC groups across Canada and held meetings in Ottawa, New Denver, Edmonton, Burnaby, Kamloops, Vernon, Kelowna, Victoria, Nanaimo, Calgary, Hamilton, Toronto, Winnipeg, Steveston, and Vancouver. Participants were encouraged to voice concerns or suggest initiatives on how the British Columbia government could address its history of discrimination and unjust actions toward our community.

"Remembering Redress by Those Who Were There: Celebrating Those Who Stood with Us in Our Need," held at the Church of the Holy Trinity in 2019, presented a unique opportunity to give thanks to those who helped make redress possible. Organized by Japanese Canadians for Social Justice, the event attracted a group of about one hundred politically minded individuals. Before lawyer and master of ceremonies

Shin Imai introduced the keynote speaker, author Joy Kogawa began with brief but poetic words of thanks. Former New Democrat leader Ed Broadbent, whose first wife was a JC, followed and reaffirmed his community support. Former MP John Brewin spoke on behalf of his father, the late Andrew Brewin, who led and represented JCs in the fight for redress. Omatsu, in her role as cochair of the NAJC's steering committee for BC Redress, gave a short update: community meeting results had been consolidated into the NAJC community consultation report and were to be presented to the government with recommendations expected before year-end.

The entire program lasted only a few hours and finished early. I stopped to thank Kogawa and mentioned our *Nikkei Voice* connection. Graciously, she said a few words before quickly departing.

"She didn't know who you were ..." Gaëtan remarked as soon as we moved out of earshot.

"I know, I've been away from the community for too long. Plus, when we were in contact it was mostly by email or phone — and rarely face-to-face," I reasoned.

About to leave, we ran into Toke Suyama waiting for his carpool. We met years ago when I worked at JSS and he was on the board. Despite his extensive career as a social worker, restaurant owner, potter, and teacher, he remained a modest man. The Toronto NAJC board member was also the older brother of my old neighbour Kunio and a long-time friend of my great-uncle. Since moving to Momiji Health Care Society, the JC facility in Scarborough for older adults, Toke had stopped driving and didn't get out much anymore. Fortunately for the Buddhist residents, the TBC ministers hold a special monthly service there.

Joy Kogawa spoke at a Toronto redress celebration held at the Church of the Holy Trinity on October 5, 2019.

"How's your uncle Tin? I haven't seen him in a while."

"He's in the same boat as you since he doesn't drive," we remarked before Toke took his leave.

Too many people become isolated from their friends as they age. Grandma never learned how to drive and still depends on family to get where she needs to go. But not everyone has this support. Those of her friends who were more independent were devastated when they could no longer drive. Too proud to ask for a lift, some gave up on going out altogether and just decided to stay home.

· · ·

Uncle Tin smiles proudly. Wearing a striped shirt, he poses for a photo with three of his grandchildren in the new temple near Downsview Park. My cousins share the spotlight, standing behind Uncle Tin and the new bronze ceremonial bell — the *kanshō* or *gyōji-shō* from Japan. It's a smaller version of the Commemorative Centennial Bell gifted to Ontario Place in 1977 but just as resonant. The photo op wasn't planned but happened by chance when Uncle Tin arrived at the right moment and bumped into the news photographer. His years of being a fixture at the temple, teaching Sunday school classes and helping at events, aligned. Grandma kept a copy of the *Toronto Star* article — "Buddhist Church Rejoices"[17] — on the dining room table to share with anyone who dropped by for a visit, proud to see her seventy-eight-year-old little brother featured in the newspaper like a celebrity.

The same *Star* article[18] showcases the light-filled new temple, which feels worlds away from its former location. From the outside the industrial-looking exterior sports a sleek block of brick and glass. Designed by church member Daniel Teramura, a principal architect with Moriyama Teshima Architects, the 18,000-square-foot open-concept interior features clean lines with repeated Japanese design elements: light panels of wood, shoji-style dividers, and narrow glass panes. Elegant in its serene simplicity, the expanded temple includes parking for eighty cars and offers more space and programs than the previous building on Bathurst Street. Events like the annual bazaar are still a big draw, and the airy spaces allow for more elbow room as huge crowds descend on the place. The sushi still sells out quickly, and patrons continue to scramble for seating in the popular downstairs dining hall during lunchtime. In the handful of services we've attended, we've grown accustomed to the chanting, respectful bowing, and offering of incense as a symbol of purification. In this entirely new building, a sense of the familiar remains.

CHAPTER 6

A TIME TO REMEMBER

There in the reed marsh
The bird sounds in sorrow
Can it be remembering
Something better to forget?
— Ki no Tsurayuki[1]

WE ALL HAVE memories we want to forget. Obon is about remembering.

Just like Catholics commemorate All Saints' Day and Mexicans celebrate the Day of the Dead, Japanese observe Obon. This annual summer Buddhist festival honours and welcomes home the spirits of one's ancestors. It is usually held mid-July but is also celebrated in August in some parts of Japan. The actual date varies depending on where you live and whether you're using the solar or lunar calendar. Some people refer to Obon as the Festival of Lanterns since it is customary to light and hang lanterns outside of one's abode to guide the spirits home. Others call it the Feast of Lanterns and enjoy a special feast during this time.

Every occasion in our family is acknowledged with lots of food — we'll take any excuse to get together and enjoy an enormous buffet of Japanese food. Unlike on New Year's Day, when traditional and auspicious foods are served, we've never had specific dishes during Obon. But since the festival happens in summer, it usually coincides with our annual family picnic in July. Many JC community groups host annual summertime picnics — it's a great opportunity to enjoy outdoor dining with some of our favourite foods. Bāchan, my great-grandmother, loved to picnic, and when summer came around, we'd pack our bento and make our way to church and community events. At Bāchan's funeral in November 1980, her son Gord suggested we meet and hold a picnic each year as a way of keeping our large family together. The following summer the entire clan gathered in her honour at Petticoat Creek Conservation Park for our first annual outing known as Bāchan's Picnic and we've been celebrating it — rain or shine — ever since. It's a day to remember Bāchan and to spend time with our extended family. Yes, it's essentially another all-day eating fest where few can resist JC favourites like onigiri, inarizushi, chow mein, soba, sliced rolls of fried egg, chicken teriyaki, sesame green beans, cooked spinach, daikon, cucumber salads, and of course, tsukemono.

After lunch there are organized activities for kids of all ages. They may vary from year to year, but you can count on straight and three-legged races, water-balloon tossing, shoe-flinging competitions, bingo, and a baseball game. To wrap things up, everyone gathers around for the share-the-wealth draws and door prizes. Usually, there are more prizes than attendees, so no one goes home empty-handed. In between all the revelry, this yearly reunion provides ample opportunities for catching up on family news and reconnecting with those who've moved away.

In the early days, we gathered in different parks around the Toronto area. Each one of Bāchan's kids set up a base where their kids clustered and shared provisions. One year when it was our turn to host, someone suggested we hold a best dessert contest. Due to the number of entries, a separate table needed to be set up for the judging. With everyone milling about, keen to sample the contenders, it encouraged more socializing. Mom's sister Irene suggested we switch to an integrated feast where everyone's contributions were laid out in a massive buffet-style luncheon. The idea stuck and we've followed suit ever since.

Imagine table after table filled with Japanese foods interspersed with picnic favourites introduced by new family members. As our family expands through intermarriage, these food traditions continue to evolve and include dishes from other cultures and nationalities. For anyone who likes sweets, there's the requisite dessert table, where you'll find the best home-baked and store-bought confections.

Our family was the first to use Caledon Place, the rural property owned by the JCCC, for our annual family picnic. In 1982, after loads of fundraising, the JCCC secured a Wintario grant and purchased a property north of Toronto in the town of Caledon. Mom happened to be a JCCC board member at the time and remembers feeling odd about making the initial request to rent the site. It opened to the public in 1985, and with the board's approval, we held Caledon Place's inaugural picnic. Others followed. Nestled among rolling hills and green pastures, those eighty-five acres became a mecca for JCs. It had everything a recreational plot should have: a thicket of woods for meandering strolls when deer flies are not around to chase you away; fields edged with wildflowers; clumps of pine trees to picnic under and escape the heat; and a series of sports areas, including a makeshift volleyball court, soccer field, and baseball diamond.

A spring-fed stream on the north end emptied into a large trout-stocked pond, luring avid fishing enthusiasts like flies about to get stuck in a web. Every year, after we arrived and unpacked our cooler and basket, Gaëtan donned his sun hat and fishing vest and wandered off alone with fly rod in hand, forgoing food, social interaction, and games. He'd spend the day blissfully casting about the water's edge and eventually returned to us by dinnertime. If not, we knew where to find him. A grassy path cut around the pond was ideal for pleasant walkabouts and provided access to the floating dock, where you'd sometimes happen on a waiting paddleboat or canoe. One end of the waterhole had a gradual slope and shallow entry point, making it an ideal beach, complete with sandy shore where young and old splashed about in the clear water on hot summer days.

On one side of the property, in an area devoid of trees, a group of volunteer gardeners had prepared the soil and cultivated a large garden patch where they sowed vegetables like corn, potatoes, onions, carrots, gobo, and daikon. During Mom's term on the JCCC board, a group of members toured the garden plot. She'll never forget the incredulous look from one of the older nisei men.

"What?! Don't you know what that is?"

"No, I don't," Mom shrugged sheepishly, shaking her head as she looked down at the growing crops.

"It's a potato plant!"

She recognized the corn stalks, but unlike the older generation of JCs, most of the names and features of agricultural staples were unfamiliar to her. Despite living on a farm in Chatham, my mom was about six and a half years old in 1947 when the family moved to Toronto. She grew up a city girl and never understood my interest in gardening. Clearly, the joy of back-breaking, sweat-inducing mucking about had skipped a generation. Luckily, the older folk like Grandma, Grandpa, Auntie Tomo, Auntie Sakae, and Auntie Irene generously shared flowers and plants when Gaëtan and I finally had our own home and garden. These relatives encouraged our hobby, and thanks to them, we gleaned much from their botanical knowledge.

Fall harvests at Caledon Place were routinely followed by work bees to make the ever-popular denba zuke–style takuwan, named after the New Denver camp. Shouldering much of this labour-intensive effort were members of the JCCC's Wynford Seniors' Club. Those who were physically able joined the working crew. Grandpa helped the men in the fields, and Grandma prepped the daikon in the kitchen with the other ladies. And as soon as these homemade pickles were ready, just like at the bazaars, jar after jar were quickly snatched up for purchase.

Our annual Bāchan's Picnic is firmly rooted in decades of family history. Average attendance each summer used to peak at around two hundred people. These days it's more like one hundred. Our older nisei have passed away or can't attend due to health reasons, and the younger generation is too busy with other commitments. I've often thought of our family as a microcosm for the larger community. Despite its initial popularity, Caledon Place experienced a decline in usage and rental fees. Mirroring the drop in our picnic attendance, aging members began to find the drive and garden work tiresome. No longer self-sufficient and facing rising maintenance costs, Caledon Place was listed for sale in 2003. A generous community member purchased it and welcomed our family to continue using the site for almost another decade. That benefactor died in 2012 but bequeathed the property back to the JCCC. Sadly, the board decided to later dispose of the property and said sayonara. Caledon Place hosted its last community picnic in the summer of 2019.

Planning a large-scale activity like our family picnic is no small undertaking. Lots of lead time is required. Each year a different family takes a turn acting as the host to ensure no particular branch of our clan is burdened with all the leg work. Bāchan had eight children, and the extended family of each child rotates through the responsibility, including choosing the picnic theme and venue. Those with smaller families have banded together to share the tasks with their combined power.

Since our picnic usually conflicts with the JCCC's Natsu Matsuri festival, some family members have advocated for a date change, but talk of altering the day has always been met with protest and resistance. In retrospect it seems fitting our annual gathering is held on the same weekend as Obon. After spending a lovely day with family and friends, those with energy to burn can make their way to the JCCC for another round of activities, including the evening *bon odori* performances. For any of our ancestors returning home in spirit, we've ensured their visit is packed full of celebrations.

• • •

Depending on the source of the Buddhist legend, the specific details on how Obon and bon odori originated vary, but the essence of the story remains the same.

One legend, in Mock Joya's series *Quaint Customs and Manners of Japan*,[2] tells of an Indian priest with supernatural powers. After his mother died, he searched for her and found her suffering for her past selfishness and starving in the underworld. He tried to offer her food, but each time, it simply turned to flame. He asked the Buddha for advice and was instructed to offer lots of food and drink to as many priests as possible and to pray for her salvation. The priest rushed to plan a grand memorial service for his mother on July 15 and invited all the priests in the area to gather and enjoy an abundance of food. With the priest's mother saved, the attending disciples celebrated this blessing and began to clap their hands and dance in joy. Another origin story[3] tells the tale of one of the Buddha's gifted disciples. This monk had some type of extraordinary sense perception, allowing him to realize the compassion of the Buddha. Overjoyed with this knowledge, he clapped his hands and danced.

The custom of dancing at Obon has continued to be a large part of the festivities. The specific style of dance performed during Obon is called bon odori, which combines the Japanese word for "dance" (odori) with the less formal version of "Obon" (bon). Regardless of which origin story one believes, Obon continues to be celebrated every summer in Japan, Canada, and elsewhere in the world.

• • •

It's important for all JCs, regardless of our beliefs, to remember, honour, and celebrate our own. Here in Canada, our lives have been enhanced thanks to the efforts of many issei and nisei, and we enjoy rights and freedoms previously denied to those community founders. One of those key individuals was Tomekichi "Tomey" Homma.[4] He believed everyone should have the right to vote regardless of their ethnic background. In 1900 he applied to have his name included on the voter registry in the Vancouver district where he lived. This challenged the British Columbia Provincial Elections Act, which barred not only women but also Asian Canadians and Indigenous Peoples from voting. His request was immediately denied. Undeterred, he decided to take Thomas Cunningham, the registrar, to court. Initially, the county court and Supreme Court of British Columbia ruled in Homma's favour, but their decision faced an appeal at the highest level. Ruling in favour of the province, the Judicial Committee of the Privy Council in London, England, later reversed the decision. Although unsuccessful, the landmark case *Cunningham v. Homma* (1903) records a time in Canadian history when a province could withhold the vote on the basis of gender and race. Remembered as one of the early pioneers of civil rights, Homma died while incarcerated in Slocan, before ever seeing his efforts come to fruition.

Leaving a life of privilege behind in Japan, an eighteen-year-old Homma arrived in Canada in 1883, eager for new freedom and opportunities. His efforts were soon recognized as he became known as a prominent community leader helping to build the local JC community and establishing many of its key organizations: the Japanese Fishermen's Benevolent Society; the Japanese Fishermen's Hospital; the first Japanese language schools in Stevenson and Vancouver; and *Canada Shimpo*, Vancouver's first Japanese daily newspaper. Homma also operated a boarding house and worked as an employment agent.

Downtown Vancouver bustled with industry centred around Hastings Mill, founded in 1865 and a major employer for new Japanese immigrants. These men worked long, hard hours at the mill and, for convenience, looked for nearby accommodations. All types of businesses sprang up to meet and cater to the workers' needs, and more immigrants like Homma arrived ready to seize these opportunities and set up enterprises: rooming houses, shops, Japanese merchants, grocers, and tradespeople. Gaining this tiny foothold along Powell Street marked the beginning of the Japanese community and led to the birth of a Japantown, often called Little Tokyo or Paueru Gai.

Unfortunately, these establishments attracted resentments from the white majority. Groups like the Asiatic Exclusion League formed to share their desire and determination to halt this growing "menace" from overtaking the country. In voicing their concerns, they planned a large anti-Asian demonstration for September 7, 1907, which began with a parade to Vancouver's city hall. Upon reaching the site, around eight thousand marchers heard heated and emotional speeches on maintaining "a white Canada." Some of the attendees formed an angry mob, breaking away from the crowd to storm Chinatown, smashing windows and looting shops.

The violent horde turned to Powell Street's Little Tokyo unaware that a group of Japanese who had been tipped off about the approach were ready and waiting for them. Ken Adachi, in *The Enemy That Never Was*, describes the harrowing scene: "The Japanese met the mob at first with defensive tactics, pelting rocks down from rooftops. But then they sallied forth with sticks, clubs, iron bars, knives and bottles. Crying 'Banzai' they tore into the mob. Some of the Japanese went to ground as stones thumped against heads, but the mob soon wavered, broke, retreated — some men gashed and bleeding, their lust for conflict quickly dissipated by the unexpected and fiery resistance."[5] Fighting continued during the next two days and culminated in an attempt to burn down the local Japanese language school.

New efforts were made to curtail Japanese immigration. The Hayashi-Lemieux "Gentleman's Agreement" in 1908 allowed Japan to voluntarily limit the number of passports issued to Japanese male labourers and domestic servants. However, since Japanese women faced no restrictions, the ban had little effect.[6] Discord created by the Asiatic Exclusion League continued to fuel tensions between the Japanese community and Caucasian majority. By the time Japan attacked Pearl Harbor in 1941, anti-Japanese sentiments were at an all-time high. With little public resistance, the local government freely petitioned for the speedy removal of all Japanese from the British Columbia coast.

Once interned, many Buddhists refused to abandon their cultural traditions. Homes and worldly possessions may have been lost but their faith remained. Uncle Tin frequented the Buddhist temple located beside the Japanese school in Slocan and remembers celebrating Obon with bon odori performances. Janet McLellan notes in *Many Petals of the Lotus*, "In Slocan, an elaborate shrine was also set up, donated from a dismantled Jodo Shinshu temple. In all other camps, however, shrines were makeshift, composed of personal items donated by the evacuees. Although Jodo Shinshu clergy were supposedly prohibited from practising, Toronto Buddhist Church members recall that regular services were still performed every Sunday, as well as services for memorials, weddings and funerals."[7]

Other camps also continued to observe basic customs and ceremonies despite harsh conditions. Internees like Toshio Mori shared memories: "In Sandon, I remember the first Bon Odori. This was soon after we settled in that town, July of 1942.… The men built a large platform in the centre of the town and the girls came down from the top of a hill dancing, the music blaring from the P.A. system. They danced around the platform and soon everyone joined in the odori. It was a time to celebrate, and despite everything terrible happening to us, we could still follow in the teachings of the Buddha."[8]

Forced relocation after the war brought many JCs to Toronto, where they founded the Toronto Young Buddhist Society (TYBS) and built the first Buddhist temple. The Fujinkai, the TBC's women's association formed in 1948, started Obon Odori and staged performances in the early 1950s as part of the TYBS summer picnics in Greenwood Conservation Park. Instruction on Japanese folk dances began in 1961 when Chiyo Seko, one of the Sakura Kai founders, started teaching the women in the TBC's Minyō Group and culminated with the first Obon performance in Christie Pits Park. Seko continued as instructor until 1965 when Susie Yoshikawa also became involved as one of the initial instructors. From Christie Pits the summer festival quickly grew in popularity and sought other performance venues, moving to Dufferin Grove Park and then to Nathan Phillips Square in front of Toronto's city hall.[9]

Seeds of discontent planted decades earlier by Tomey Homma finally blossomed one spring when voting rights were granted to JCs with the passing of Bill 43 in the British

Mom and Auntie Irene dancing in the 1950s.

Columbia legislature on April 1, 1949.[10] Community momentum began to build and flourish. Greater racial and religious tolerance led to inspired action. JCs were no longer inhibited by unjust laws, and they pressed forward to regain lost ground and establish firm roots in Toronto. Progressive concepts emerged as the 1960s challenged traditional ideas, ushering in antiwar sentiments, the push to empower women and people of colour, and a desire to integrate other cultures and religions. A growing counterculture rejected the rigid social norms of the past and encouraged exploration of other spiritual concepts like Zen philosophies and Buddhism. During this time the TBC went through many changes. Rev. Newton Ishiura and his wife, Mary, replaced founding minister Rev. Tsuji, who retired in 1958. The Ishiuras' progressive ideas were welcomed during this time of social change.[11]

In the bigger picture, Canada's former immigration laws controlling the flow of "undesirable races" were finally changed in 1967, and within the next few years, Canada began its initial forays into multiculturalism — what became a defining feature for large cities like Toronto. "The new immigration laws after 1967 were race-neutral and based on points — points for the level of education, ability to speak one of the national languages, type of occupation, etc. Those with enough points, regardless of race, were allowed to immigrate. In the 1970s under the government of Pierre Elliott Trudeau, Canada adopted a policy of multiculturalism, officially welcoming people of all races and cultures."[12]

No longer content to simply assimilate into mainstream culture, JC parents looked for avenues to expose their third-generation children to their ethnic heritage as a way of maintaining customs and traditions. Some of these sansei kids had no knowledge of what it meant to be Japanese. Creative outlets for young people sprang up to fill this void, organizations like the Sakura Kai and Sansei Choir. Fuelled by their founders' passion for dance and music, these groups were led by individuals versed in traditional Japanese culture and the arts. Both groups performed at the opening of the newly built community hub, the JCCC, in 1963.

The TBC's Minyō Group continued to welcome and encourage all members of the JC community to participate in the annual Obon performances, and other dance troupes soon joined: the Sakura Kai and Haru-Yagi Kai dancers from the JCCC in Toronto and members from Hamilton's Buddhist Church and Suzuran-Kai. Church member and one-time president of the TYBS Kunio Suyama distinguished himself at these events by becoming the regular MC. A new tradition was born, one we were soon to become a part of. The JC community made its mark by infusing the Toronto landscape with unique structures and organizations — a legacy and testament to its unwavering commitment and perseverance.

• • •

Have you ever heard a song and suddenly been transported back to another place in time? For me it's the "Tankō Bushi," or "Coal Miner's Dance," with its unmistakable twang of the shamisen, a Japanese lute. Immediately, I'm wearing a cotton *yukata* (summer kimono) and dancing during Obon.

Just like a certain smell can stir a long-forgotten memory, music can have a powerful effect on the brain. Many people associate "memory music" with a specific era and on hearing a particular song from that time, are instantly reminded of a key event or milestone. Like riding a bike, there's muscle memory, too, which somehow remembers the motions of tasks or, in my case, steps to traditional Japanese folk dances learned decades ago. Case in point: it may have been years since I first learned the "Tankō Bushi," but somehow, it's remained permanently ingrained in me, unlike other dances I've learned over the years.

As a young girl, I used to think Obon was just about dancing, what we called *minyō*. That word, I discovered later, refers to the genre of Japanese folk music accompanying bon odori, but it can also mean folk dance or nostalgia. Bon odori provided my introduction to Japanese dancing. Easy to learn, these rhythmic dances comprised of repetitive steps are performed during Obon. Similar to classical dance, each one tells a story, but instead of performing on stage with elaborate costumes or silk kimono, dancers from young to old form circles (usually outdoors) and wear *yukata*. According to the TBC website, "Every region in Japan has its own particular dances and kinds of music. Sometimes fans, long cotton towels, sticks, or castanets are used. Hand gestures and movements show different aspects of life, such as coal mining, fishing or harvesting rice, or nature, such as blooming flowers or flowing rivers."[13]

Long before the large, lighted sign that screams "TORONTO" presided over Nathan Phillips Square, my mother took us downtown to watch her sister Norma dance during Obon. We were immediately captivated as we stood amid city hall and the legislative buildings on that summer day. Round and round in circles, dance after dance, performers in eye-catching, brightly coloured kimono moved effortlessly to Japanese music punctuated by the rhythmic pounding of taiko drums, sounds that carried through the air like thunder. So much to take in.

The big finale culminated with an invitation from our neighbour Mr. Suyama. Acting as the MC, he encouraged the audience to join the festivities by participating in the "Tankō Bushi." Without hesitation we jumped in as he explained the meaning behind the dance moves and walked us novices through the motions: they began with digging and carrying,

The next generation of sisters to dance during the summer Obon festival at Nathan Phillips Square in the 1970s.

followed by the wiping of the brow, and finished with the emptying of the gathered coal into a bin. A clap of the hands and the work started again. Whether it was the thrill of performing with the large crowd or the delight in a fun family outing, from that moment on we were hooked. By the next year, Mom had signed us up for odori lessons.

After the performance we skipped over to Dundas Street for dinner at Sai Woo restaurant. Piling into the lively Chinese hub, we climbed into our seats at round tables and shared dishes fit for an Obon-inspired feast. In those days Japanese restaurants were few and far between — mostly formal and expensive places where you'd be greeted with hot towels to wash your hands. On rare occasions when we went to a restaurant, our family headed to Sai Woo in Chinatown or uptown to China House on Eglinton Avenue West.

Months passed before my sister and I found ourselves in the basement of the TBC on Bathurst Street. Right away, at the first dance practice with the TBC's Minyō Group, I noticed there weren't many kids my age. Nor were there any mixed kids like us. Searching the crowd of mostly older Japanese women, we found familiar faces in our great-aunties Nellie, Kay, and Sakae and a few younger people, including Auntie Norma, cousins Eleanor and Pam, and our neighbours Debbie and Julie.

Looking across the large space one practice, my eyes widened when I saw Kimiko. She looked like a *kokeshi* doll with her straight black hair and bangs cut into a perfect bob. Small and pretty, she already seemed to know most of the steps and moved with the fluidity of a more experienced dancer. I remember feeling awkward and embarrassed, an out-of-place, funny-looking kid totally lacking in grace. Stumbling along clumsily beside my new friend each practice, I did my best to learn the dances by mimicking her every move. With her palm up and outstretched arm moving to the beat of the music, I caught sight of her delicate hands and smooth tanned skin, so unlike my own. Suddenly, I felt all gangly and white.

Even though I was among people with whom I identified the most, it wouldn't be the last time I felt like an outsider. I may have grown more "white passing" with age, but unlike my Caucasian contemporaries, I never felt I blended in with either side, no matter how much I wanted to or how hard I tried. As a child I didn't understand why I had these hurtful feelings or how to express them. In that moment of self-consciousness, I became aware of the fact I was different. And for the first time, a new thought entered my mind: *If only I were more Japanese-looking.*

Years of being gawked at, like some type of freak show attraction, helped me develop an inner resilience — a boldness even. Slowly, I've grown more comfortable in my own skin. At some point I finally accepted there's no escape. I could hang my head in shame for the apparent crime of being born of mixed race or fiercely face all opposition unapologetically. Thankfully, I've moved past the stage where I feel obliged to answer every inane question just to be polite or allow it to upset me. But sooner or later, there's always someone who'll ask, "What are you?" I'm still human, the last time I checked. Flippant retorts aside, this is who I am. Decades of questioning my identity motivated me to build a sturdy foundation in the face of adversity, like the generations before me. Understanding my culture and family history, and celebrating it in all its imperfections, has a way of bolstering strength. It is the fuel that continues to drive me forward. Whatever our background, I'm of the firm belief we should teach our children to accept and embrace who they are from an early age. As adults we can benefit from these lessons, too, instead of feeling the need to compartmentalize ourselves into tidy boxes to make it easier for other people to label us. Each one of us is unique, and just like our fingerprints, our true identity lies within, regardless of any effort we may make to deny or alter our appearance. It's our differences that define us and make us who we are.

CHAPTER 7

HEART AND SOUL

WE PULL INTO the driveway and sail through the wide open gate. It's a striking contrast. Most days the entrance is off-limits — firmly latched and chained shut. Turning down the sloped incline, we swing past the stone sculpture that stands smack dab in front of a distinctive landmark building and pull into an adjacent parking spot. For more than half a century, those stones have marked a two-storey study in concrete and wood, the entrance to 123 Wynford Drive.

Stepping out of the car, my husband and I make our way across the asphalt. Suddenly, I'm hit by a wave of nostalgia. Everything seems so familiar, yet each subtle change forces me to pause and reflect for a moment. Trees and shrubs have taken root around the stone sculpture, and a new metal sign has been posted: "Please Keep off Statue." The art installation *Tein-en* by

Raymond Moriyama is a mountainous pile of stone made from long slabs of pockmarked rock. It looks as if giant hands, in a single circular swipe, smoothed down a towering stack of dove-grey dominos to lay almost flat on the ground. Propped up in the middle, a few of the rectangular pieces of rock lean edge to edge against one another and loosely form a standing circle.

If you look for it, you'll find a hidden space at the top. Like a gap in a toothy grin, a low spot in the rock circle provides access to a platform that sits below the rim and isn't visible from the outside. We discovered it when we were kids. Although it was frowned upon, as mischievous brats we'd race up and around the outer ring of those deeply creviced stones. Once we reached the top, we'd pause to make sure no one was looking before stealthily making a quick leap over and instantly becoming invisible in plain sight. It felt magical being encircled by rock with only the open sky above us to ponder, sitting all quiet and serene inside that secret cave. What a great place to hide.

"See, it's still there," I motioned to my husband as we walked around the sculpture. I could see my childhood friend peeking through a crack between two large rocks on this sunny and humid afternoon in September. We're back to visit the place where it all happened — the place of my youth.

. . .

The original Japanese Canadian Cultural Centre — often dubbed the JCCC or simply the Centre — was a site of annual events, special guest visits, countless weddings, and weekly lessons. Though hard to fathom the Centre without the stone marker, it came later during the garden-and-landscaping stage and wasn't present when the facility opened to the public. After the board commissioned a young nisei to design its inaugural building, the JCCC was built in 1963. For the fledgling architect Moriyama, this project cemented the start of what became a remarkable career.

Despite Moriyama's newbie status at the time, his efforts garnered interest from the design community. Included with the JCCC program for the official opening was a pamphlet outlining distinct structural features, reprinted from a spread in *Canadian Architect*. In the magazine's March 1964 edition, architect Macy DuBois, who designed the Ontario Pavilion at Expo 67, provided a critical but nevertheless approving appraisal of the building:

> Vitality and conviction are conspicuous qualities of Raymond Moriyama's Japanese Canadian Cultural Centre, and one senses that it was done by an architect who believes that architecture can rise above utility and provide a rich focus to life … the building still has an impressive total impact and gives the feeling of an artifact, well placed by an architect with a pleasing textural sense. It is one of several recent ones by other architects as well which are so affecting Toronto that one can only suppose the architecture in Canada is beginning to rise to the level of the best of world architecture. These buildings do not have a stylistic tie, but rather one of excellence and conviction.[1]

The heat of summer had yet to set in that evening on June 7, 1964. A mass of men in suits and ladies donning fashionable hats and spring coats slowly filed into the parking lot outside the JCCC. Some stood while others settled into chairs, waiting for the program to begin at seven o'clock. On the veranda beside the main entrance sat three rows of Eames-style stackable side chairs. Facing out, they had the effect of a makeshift stage allowing for many vantage points during the proceedings. Visiting dignitaries offered their remarks, including Rev. Minoru Takada, JCCC president Sam "Masami" Hagino, Ambassador of Japan Nobuhiko Ushiba, and Canada Japan Society president Seijiro Yoshizawa. The keynote speaker, Prime Minister Lester B. Pearson, positioned himself behind the wooden podium and addressed the large assembly. Maryon Pearson, wearing white gloves and a cropped fur cape draped over a black dress, listened attentively as her husband unveiled a commemorative plaque that remained on display for decades:

> **In Commemoration**
> Upon this Cultural Centre we bestow all our consideration for the Issei, whose pioneer life in Canada is acknowledged in this embracement, and therefrom the inspiration to the Nisei and following generations to seek enrichment through their cultural heritage, that they may share the benefits of this interest with all Canadians.

Auntie Marlene, one of my mother's younger sisters, still remembers that day. As one of about nineteen children who comprised the Sansei Choir, she stood wearing a bold floral-striped kimono and waited for the cue from conductor Harry Kumano.

Lifting his hands in the signal to begin, the unmistakable melody of the folk song rang out:

> *Sakura, sakura* (Cherry blossoms, cherry
>   blossoms)
> *yayoi no sora wa* (Across the spring sky)
> *mi watasu kagiri* (As far as the eye can see)
> *kasumi ka kumo ka* (Is it a mist? Is it a cloud?)
> *nioi zo izuru* (Their fragrance fills the air)
> *izaya izaya* (Come now, come now)
> *mi ni yukan* (Let's go and see them)

At the time, Marlene was one month shy of her thirteenth birthday. She remembers throngs of people eager to tour the building and view the exhibits following the formal proceedings. Pressing through the crowd, she made her way to the prime minister and asked for his autograph. Marked with signatures from Pearson and Ushiba, her now yellowed program outlines how building the Centre began as a promise:

> If the growth from seed to fruition has
> been strewn with difficulties, it is only a
> reflection, writ small of the process which
> the Issei pioneers have undergone in their
> efforts to carve a life for themselves and
> their progeny in Canada. And it is to the
> Issei that this Centre is commemorated as
> a living memorial, one which will endure
> as a reminder and an inspiration for many
> generations to come.[2]

From its humble roots as a site catering to JCs, the JCCC evolved to serve all Canadians. To extend this idea, it created the motto "Friendship Through Culture" and held a competition to design a special logo. The winning design, by Stanley Shikatani, featured two vertically stacked halves of a circle and symbolized a new unity.

• • •

The Sansei Choir was a Toronto-based group founded in 1963 by nisei singer and actor Harry Kumano, and it started as a musical and social outlet for sansei children between the ages of five and twelve years. Before and after the JCCC on Wynford Drive officially opened, the group practised every Sunday in one of the lower-level rooms. Auntie Marlene, one of the original members, remembers Kumano fondly: "He wanted the sansei generation to feel connected to their heritage, so he decided to form a children's choir and teach them Japanese children's songs. He knew many sansei could not read, write, or even understand Japanese, but he knew the ability of music to transcend ethnicity, and that the language of music speaks to everyone."

Using performance as its means of initiation, the Sansei Choir introduced many Canadians to Japanese culture, including its own participants. Their young voices charmed audiences of all ages. Before long the choir became a beacon in leading families to the Centre. In their roles as founders, members, and tireless volunteers, these parents and their children made enormous contributions to the community. By involving themselves in different groups and organizations, they bolstered the Centre, the JC community, and beyond. I don't think I ever met Kumano, but by starting the choir, his efforts later inter-sected with my own life in countless ways.

Auntie Marlene's handmade songbook has discoloured with age and the cardboard front cover is stained with a half moon — a brown ring from a coffee cup or perhaps a can of pop. On the bottom right-hand corner, "Sansei Choir" is print-ed in black marker. The small booklet appears to have been made from a file folder for index cards. Inside, printed on single sheets of paper and secured with a worn steel prong fastener, English lyrics to more than twenty Japanese folk songs have been typed phonetically. How many of these booklets Kumano manually assembled is unknown, but they're a testament to his desire to share his love of music and singing. He would have needed at least a dozen for his first group of students, who were gleaned from family, friends, and acquaintances.

Kumano knew Auntie Terry from Vancouver when he worked for her father at Yama Taxi, before she met and married Uncle George. After being incarcerated in Tashme, near Hope, British Columbia, Kumano's family later moved to Toronto, where they lived in East York and owned a convenience store. His mother frequented the Konko Church and became good friends with Mrs. Tomotsugu, Auntie Harumi's mother. When Kumano put the word out he wanted to form a children's choir, several relatives were keen to enlist their kids, and my cousins Gail, Dianne, Yoshimi, and Hiroshi also joined in.

Performances at the JCCC's annual events remained the choir's mainstay, although several prestigious opportunities included singing for Prince and Princess Mikasa during their visit to the JCCC in 1965; the Nationbuilders festival at the Canadian National Exhibition (CNE) from 1966 to 1969; the Ontario Folk Arts Festival at Maple Leaf Gardens in May 1967, graced by Princess Alexandra; and the 1973 CNE Grandstand, attended by Queen Elizabeth II and Prince Philip.

The choir underwent many evolutions. Instructors changed and members came and went. Kumano acted as the first volunteer director and conductor until around 1970. In 1966 a young Seiji Ozawa stepped in to assist him for a brief stint. Already an assistant conductor and music director at the time, Ozawa went on to world renown, most notably leading the Boston Symphony Orchestra. Thanks to Ozawa, the singers were given an updated look, a makeover of sorts, when he generously donated funds to purchase seafoam-grey-and-white fabric from Japan. The singers transformed into a professional-looking troupe, their mishmash of family-owned or borrowed kimono replaced with matching ensembles fashioned from that maple leaf–patterned material.

Group members debuted their new kimono on August 5 at the Expo 67 Ontario Day celebration. To the delight of the Montreal audience, their dramatic entrance featured tiny dancers emerging from specially built miniature pavilions positioned high on the Place des Nations tiered steps. Standing below them and wearing the new kimono with matching golden obi and navy-and-white zori sandals, each singer held an identical orange-and-white fan. Singing in unison, they produced a chorus line effect. About six thousand people greeted the group with cheers. During the second stanza of the song "Sakura," Auntie Marlene launched into her solo. She remembers being amazed at the massive crowd: "It was a solid sea of people as far as the eye could see, with no end."

Following these centennial events, which included an August 1967 performance of "Wonderful Canada" at the CNE's Nationbuilders folk festival, Kumano received a thank-you letter from Premier John P. Robarts. Congratulating Kumano for the choir's role in making Expo 67 a success, Robarts invited all the Ontario Day show performers to attend a reception on August 30, 1967, on the front lawn of the legislative buildings at Queen's Park. Each member of the choir received a certificate and a boxed set of two commemorative medallions. In a show of thanks, Kumano and choir president Tad Morishita presented Allan Grossman, minister of reform institutions, with a copy of the 45 rpm record "Wonderful Canada."

When local dance instructor Chiyo Seko agreed to teach odori to the five- and six-year-old members, the choir changed their name to Sansei Choir and Dancers. Now young dancers performed alongside the choir, adding to the attraction of sweet singing voices. Ever-popular numbers such as "Sho Jo Ji" ("Badgers Song") featured the tots dressed in animal costumes, acting out song lyrics as they moved to the music. A ten-year-old Auntie Norma, the youngest of Mom's sisters, decided to step in and become one of the earliest dancers. For several years she danced, long after her sister Marlene had left the group.

• • •

Resembling a Japanese Buddy Holly, with his signature black-frame glasses, musician and composer Akira "Archie" Nishihama became involved with the Sansei Choir when he composed and released "Canada Ondo," written in honour of Canada's centennial year.

Born in Vancouver, a young Nishihama dreamed of becoming a recording star. In 1939 the five-year-old, his mother, and his siblings set sail for Japan. His father remained behind at their Britannia Beach home, but once the uprooting of JCs started was removed to a work camp in Lempriere, British Columbia, and then one in Toronto. Nishihama went on to study music at Osaka's Music School of Japan. During this time he met singers from the Nippon Mercury Record Co., and the talented vocalist began performing onstage. One morning in 1955, the twenty-two-year-old suffered a lung hemorrhage and his career visions faded before him. He decided to pursue other options and, after a ten-year separation, reunited with his father in Canada. His mother joined them the following year.

The Maple Leaf Cultural Association in Tokyo sponsored a musical tribute contest, and on August 30, 1966, the *Continental Times* reported Nishihama's score was selected as the winning entry. Setsuko Higashi of Japan wrote the English lyrics selected to accompany it. News of Nishihama's success spread. By October 11, 1966, a notice posted in the same paper indicated the Sansei Choir was looking for new members and stated, "Director Harry Kumano is anxious to start on the 'Canada Ondo' selected as a Centennial theme song" and "composer Mr. Archie Nishihama will attend and assist the choir in its presentation."[3]

Back in Japan, for reasons unknown, Nishihama's score was pushed aside by the Maple Leaf Cultural Association and two new songs titled "Wonderful Canada," one English and one Japanese, were produced and recorded as a 45 rpm record. Sporting maple leaves, the colourful "Wonderful Canada" record sleeve included an insert with English lyrics and photo-illustrated dance instructions choreographed by Tokubei Hanayagi. The back cover reads like a pulp-and-paper ad. It features a list of products and news of a pulp mill being built in Skookumchuck, British Columbia, by Honshu Paper Manufacturing Co. in Tokyo and their Canadian affiliate

Crestbrook Forest Industries in Vancouver. Japanese composer and guitarist Masao Koga, whose work was later featured in the films *Come See the Paradise* and *Memoirs of a Geisha*, was credited with writing the music. The English song uses Setsuko Higashi's lyrics, and the Japanese version is a translation. Both recordings are accompanied by the Antonio Koga Columbia Orchestra.

Unimpressed by this flashy sponsored production, Nishihama teamed up with JC musician Sam Miya to produce his own 45 rpm record. Nishihama's son Mark explains, "This association decided not to use their music for the Canadian Centennial celebration. My dad got upset and he wrote his own lyrics to go with the musical score, which he already composed … 'Canada Ondo' was born."[4] Nishihama's promising career as a vocalist had ended decades earlier, but undeterred by his previous illness, he was determined to sing again. He recorded "Canada Ondo: Our Wonderful Canada" and another original song, "Oriental Sunset," on the flip side. Garnering praise from the community, the record sold for $1.25 a copy. The *New Canadian* reported: "The Japanese Canadian recording of the J.C. Centennial Committee approved *Canada Ondo* — a song and dance in honour of Canada's Centennial — has already sold over 500 copies in the first two weeks it has been out. This Nisei version of 'Canada Ondo' is sung by its creator, talented J.C. musician Archie Nishihama of Toronto.… Five hundred more recordings have been ordered to fill the demand."[5]

Dancer Irene Tsujimoto quickly choreographed a commemorative odori to accompany "Canada Ondo." Throughout the centennial year, numerous song and dance performances followed. The JCCC's annual Spring Festival in March included the song in the Sansei Choir program. A parade down

Archie Nishihama and his wife at Toronto City Hall during the Canadian Centennial celebrations, July 1967. Uncle Tin with his camera in the background.

Yonge Street in July featured 150 dancers on the JC float. Huge crowds packed Nathan Phillips Square on July 8, 1967, for the annual Obon festival, organized in part by the Japanese Canadian Citizens' Association (JCCA) centennial committee. According to the *Continental Times*,[6] Nishihama's performance of "Canada Ondo" highlighted the event. Nishihama, dashing in a white tuxedo jacket and black bow tie, greeted the audience. As his voice rang out, more than two hundred kimono-clad dancers from local and remote dance groups accompanied him, waving Canadian and centennial flags as they performed Tsujimoto's bon odori.

Auntie Marlene's Sansei Choir songbook includes Nishihama's lyrics for "Oriental Sunset," but "Canada Ondo" is missing. Some singers remember performing the song and being given separate sheet music, although the ones I found in Marlene's files were mislabelled and matched the Japanese lyrics for "Wonderful Canada." If Nishihama harboured any ill will from the song switch, he never revealed it and continued to include "Wonderful Canada" in the choir's repertoire when he became conductor.

Nishihama replaced Kumano as conductor in 1970, and Hiroshi "Phil" Katayama succeeded him from 1971 to 1972 until family commitments called him away. Nishihama returned to the helm following Katayama's departure to guide the choir until the final curtain fell in 1974. Rather than fading to black, the show went on for some of the performers, like Auntie Norma, when they turned exclusively to dance. Odori teacher Mrs. Seko taught for a short period and was succeeded in 1967 by Harumi Nakamura, who continued to provide dance lessons. Once the singers disbanded, Auntie Harumi renamed the dance troupe Haru-Yagi Kai.

Various dance groups continued to perform both "Wonderful Canada" and "Canada Ondo" during summer festivals. Years later, after the Obon Odori merged with Natsu Matsuri at the JCCC, Nishihama's work was celebrated again at the July 2017 festival. Following the evening bon odori performances, which included both dances, the TBC's Obon Odori committee presented a commemorative plaque to Nishihama's family for his song "Canada Ondo." Sadly, he suffered a fatal brain aneurysm in December 1996 and did not live to see this honour.

During the Covid-19 pandemic and lockdown measures in 2020, Natsu Matsuri was cancelled, but this didn't stop the JC community from sharing fond Obon recollections on social media. A debate surfaced between dancers, singers, and other community members regarding Canada's centennial events in 1967. Though many remembered Nishihama from the choir, many believed the song "Wonderful Canada" had eclipsed "Canada Ondo." Some people were adamant and remembered the two different songs and dances. Others thought they were one and the same. Had they remembered wrong? Memory is a funny thing.

The two songs may share similar themes but couldn't be more different. "Wonderful Canada" is a peppy march sung with a female and a male lead in alternating stanzas and includes backing vocals. It features both a Japanese and English version recorded in Japan by Japanese musicians. "Canada Ondo" is slower paced and features Nishihama's solo vocals and Japanese lyrics. It was made in Canada by JCs. One Canadian, one Japanese — the two divides for many JCs. For Nishihama these elements played strong roles in shaping his life. His creative efforts intersected with two centennial tributes, which he leaves as part of his musical contributions to Canada. For a time, Nishihama's rising star burned brightly.

• • •

There is always someone who leads the group in song, whether it's a celebratory version of "Happy Birthday," a wedding ode, or a sombre funeral hymn. Our family songbird has always been Auntie Marlene. Singled out to perform the only solos during her days in the Sansei Choir, Marlene's distinctive alto continues to cut through the crowd at any family function.

Marlene had always been my cool aunt. Back in the early 1970s, she and her group of friends regularly planted themselves in the living room on Browning Avenue. I remember her old boyfriend Oleg. He had long blond hair, wore turtlenecks and corduroy bell bottoms, and played the guitar while she, in her crochet vest, sang their favourite songs. Rather than dismiss a curious child awestruck by the music, the young adults kindly welcomed me whenever I crept down from the third floor and edged my way into the room. Later, as a young teen, I cherished the amazing vintage clothing and accessories Marlene generously passed down to me. Despite being raised by a single mother, my sister and I never lacked stylish clothes. One time when I visited Auntie Marlene at her apartment, she offered me a cigarette — the one and only relative to ever do so. "I know you smoke," she laughed.

Over the years Auntie Marlene documented the Sansei Choir's activities and probably has one of the most extensive collections of memorabilia. On July 6, 2013, the JCCC celebrated their fifty-year anniversary and invited current club members to join them for a special Nostalgia Night. Auntie Marlene was asked to organize something on behalf of the choir, but the committee member made it clear there wasn't room for anything to be included in the formal program. Disappointed, she learned the event organizers were unfamiliar with the now-defunct choir and the pivotal role its members and their families had played in the community. She made a point of mentioning how the choir performed at the Centre's opening celebration to another one of the Nostalgia Night committee members. In light of this information and at the last minute, the choir was invited to perform an encore of "Sakura."

Due to space constraints, tickets to the catered dinner were capped at four hundred and quickly sold out. Those who weren't able to attend the sit-down supper could check out the booths set up in the JCCC foyer for the general public during the day or take part in the beer garden activities later that evening. Each JCCC-based club or group was encouraged to set up a booth in the lobby to showcase their activities with an array of photos or archives for patrons to peruse. Marlene hunted down former members to gather information and additional materials and managed to prepare five photo-filled scrapbooks for the event, which she proudly displayed at the Sansei Choir table.

In one of the books, Auntie Marlene and cousin Gail cowrote a brief history of the club. More than anything, they wanted to document and acknowledge the role parents played in driving the members to every practice, event, and function. Not only did these dedicated parents donate money, but they also developed fundraising activities and other countless events by volunteering years of their time and "helped build the JCCC into one of the largest and most vibrant Japanese culture centres in the world." The printed account includes the following words of appreciation: "Thank you to the parents, for all you have done, for enriching our lives by exposing us to our Japanese heritage, and for inspiring us, the sansei, to continue to volunteer and participate in the clubs and events at the JCCC. We hope to influence the next generations — the yonsei, gosei, ijūsha — so they will be the next ambassadors of 'Friendship Through Culture' in Canada and beyond."

On the afternoon of the big day, Auntie Marlene cheerfully greeted guests and reconnected with old friends. She tried to contact all the original sixty-one participants of the choir. For the dinner, she reserved tables and turned the event into a mini reunion. She smuggled in a handful of family members to attend the presentation, and we were quick to usher ourselves out once it was over. On stage in Kobayashi Hall, a group of about twenty former choir members stood in formation after a four-decade hiatus; they were no longer kids but a pack of middle-aged adults. Projected over the width of the stage, on a screen behind the performers, was a photo of them as children.

Permitted to say a few words on behalf of the choir, Marlene congratulated the JCCC on reaching this fifty-year milestone. She named those who had already passed away: founder Harry Kumano, conductor Archie Nishihama, and odori instructor Harumi Nakamura. She also paid tribute to their extended families, including dance instructor Mrs. Seko and all the choir members' parents, whether alive or in memory: "We the sansei now as adults realize we owe a huge debt of gratitude to some very special dedicated people ... without these people's tireless efforts to teach us, we would not have the experiences and fond memories of our childhood. We thank you and would like to acknowledge your contributions."

Former conductors Kumano and Nishihama had not lived to see this joyful reunion. In their place Phil Katayama agreed to lead the group, mere hours before the performance. His daughter Amie had been reluctant to commit because her father had begun to show early signs of Alzheimer's. Driving to the Centre that evening, Amie asked her father, "Would you like to conduct the choir tonight?" Deeply honoured at the request, Katayama agreed.

During Marlene's introduction of Katayama, Amie and choir member Marty Kobayashi quietly exited the stage to help the conductor up the stairs to join the group. Wearing a cheerful yellow-check shirt and ivory chinos, the gaunt eighty-one-year-old moved slowly, but he carried himself with a stately posture, stopping to lean on his black-handled cane with every step for balance. Ceremoniously bowing his bald head to address the crowd, Katayama moved deliberately with short steps and turned to face the singers. With a cue to returning member and piano player Gail Kitamura, the silence was filled with a few solitary and distinct notes of "Sakura." The choir joined in tentatively, gaining volume and tone as Katayama's conducting grew more vigorous. Midway into the song, he began marking certain lyrics with fully extended arms and strong gestures. By the end of the second stanza, his cane dangled off one arm. To signal the finale, he firmly raised both hands triumphantly in a strong flourish.

The crowd erupted into applause as the former students bowed respectfully before their old sensei. Facing the singers, Katayama returned their gesture with a short nod of approval. With his back to the crowd, the audience didn't see his eyes had filled with tears. And throughout the performance, though it may have escaped the seated patrons, many of the singers from the opposite vantage point noticed him struggle to maintain his composure. Shuffling around, Phil Katayama bowed before the audience for one last time.

• • •

Sold in July 2001, 123 Wynford Drive became a centre for Islamic practice and learning known as the Noor Cultural Centre. On September 22, 2019, they cancelled their regular Sunday program and graciously opened their doors to the JC community.

At first I second-guess myself as I double take on entering the main doors. *Wait a minute, these handles have been re-made.* It's uncanny how closely they resemble the ones that used to be there. The only difference? One telltale giveaway — they're engraved with the Arabic word "noor." I remind myself, *I'm not imagining things.* This motif, repeated throughout the building, is remarkably similar to the JCCC logo the former doors once sported.

Rows of tables and chairs line the front of the stage in the main auditorium with more chairs set up behind them. Settling in close to the front, I glance around the auditorium and quickly spot a few familiar faces. JCCC past president Marty Kobayashi is seated at a table on the opposite side of us, with his daughter and son-in-law. I notice a stylish white-haired man at the back of the large room, wearing a blue-print shirt, zipped tan sweater, and grey pants with white-soled black sneakers. Even from a distance, he's instantly recognizable as the architect Raymond Moriyama. Accompanied by JCCC president Gary Kawaguchi, he poses for the event photographer and continues to mill about, shaking hands with guests before casually strolling up to the stage. A black curtain forms the backdrop to the stark scene of two armless chairs sitting centre stage, separated by a small black table and flanked by standing microphones. There's nothing to distract from this informal interview between Moriyama and Elsa Lam, editor of *Canadian Architect* magazine. Positioned to one side is a wooden podium, where Samira Kanji, president of the Noor Cultural Centre, warmly greets the crowd of about one hundred people and congratulates the community on this thirty-first anniversary of redress, an auspicious day for a walk down memory lane.

I should have known this, I tell myself, but it had slipped my notice. Remembering key dates and historical facts was never among my strong points. Luckily, the organizers were more mindful and specifically planned the open house to coincide with this occasion. What better way to celebrate than by visiting the original JCCC and having a conversation with its architect?

· · ·

Reflecting on the Islamic community's aspirations for their centre, Kanji explained how they came to choose the name "Noor." In Arabic, the word means "light" and represents spiritual enlightenment. It also happened to be the name of her mother, family matriarch Noorbanu. According to Kanji, when her late father, philanthropist Hassanali Lakhani, toured the building in 2001, it was love at first sight. Immediately, he felt drawn to the building and decided then and there — he wanted it to be their new Islamic centre. As he learned more about how it came to be built, he cherished its history. The next challenge soon presented itself: how to convert the architectural gem into a spiritual centre.

"He had found a *Mona Lisa*, so it only made sense to call on da Vinci to make the necessary changes," Kanji stated matter-of-factly. Shortly after purchasing the building, they commissioned Moriyama Teshima Architects. To adapt the masterpiece, Kanji wanted Moriyama himself to oversee the renovations to meet Noor's objectives and ensure a seamless transition. In a nod to its namesake, the light theme carried forward, informing the design both physically and metaphorically:

> A sense of spirituality and harmony transcending cultural differences pervades the building and is felt immediately.... One of the themes for the renovation, therefore, was to enhance the quality of light already present in the building. One of the main strategies was to use wood screens to alter the quality of light. The architects designed a variety of screens incorporating ancient Arabic calligraphy. The two lanterns at the building's main façade now have screens with the words Allah Noor. A large wood screen, again with calligraphy, is installed along the exterior window of the new prayer hall and is lit at night. This new screen at the building's base is aligned exactly with the existing vertical screening above. These subtle details allude to Islamic building traditions yet are well suited to the building's architecture.[7]

Minimal changes were made to the structure, including much-needed accessibility features such as a ramp and elevator, allowing the space to be used for different purposes. The building has since become a study in adaptive reuse.

After her welcome, Kanji turned things over to Lam and Moriyama. In their conversation Moriyama explained how, as a twenty-eight-year-old architect "too young to know any better," he wanted to create symbolic architecture at a low cost with a tight budget set at fourteen dollars per square foot. During the war JCs lost everything. In regaining their freedom, reclaiming self-respect became equally important, and part of this included finding a gathering place. Location was critical. Years of fundraising and community-wide campaigns to find a suitable site for a community centre finally ended in 1961 when the JCCC's board of directors purchased the three-acre wooded lot in Don Mills. Before contract tenders could be considered or any construction begin, there remained a major shortfall. A mortgage followed by a short-term bank loan was necessary, which stipulated repayment guarantors. No one had any money in those days, and Moriyama remembered feeling grateful when seventy-five JCs stepped forward to sign the mortgage. With funds in hand, the plans were revised and tender accepted. Former Toronto mayor Nathan Phillips joined in as they broke ground with a ceremonial sod-turning in September 1962.

Moriyama's unique concept involved a pagoda-like structure nestled among the trees, reminiscent of the treehouse he'd secretly built as a child after being uprooted to Slocan. An accident as a toddler left him badly scalded, and he became self-conscious of his scars when other children in the bathhouse marked him as a leper. Outside of the incarceration camp, the nearby secluded forests were a magical place, full of life and lessons. Far from the cruel mocking, his treehouse refuge provided the perfect hideaway — a haven from the storm.

In a way I think the building represented safety and security, which were coveted by displaced people looking for a safe house and a fresh start. For me the Centre always provided a sense of comfort and familiarity. A second home filled with the faces of family, neighbours, and friends. Likewise, the building became a mecca for JCs to gather, establish roots, and find solace. A sanctuary where Japanese culture could flourish, it became a stabilizing focal point for a scattered community of survivors.

Moriyama travelled to Japan and returned with innovative ideas. While the building incorporated the simplicity of traditional Japanese design, he acknowledged how it is uniquely JC. Embracing Canadian technology, he built the structure inexpensively from eleven large concrete blocks. "Wherever possible, we tried to protect the wood," Moriyama recollected, which blended age-old Japanese ideas with modern Canadian practicality. Moriyama cited the economic drainage solution that replaced rainwater leaders as an example. Utilizing the water feature on the northwestern end of the site, strategically positioned heavy metal chains drain and direct water from the roof into a meandering creek. Beautiful and decorative in form yet highly functional, rain chains known as *kusari doi* have been used for centuries in Japanese gardens and architecture.

In his discussion of the two-storey auditorium, Moriyama pointed to the sides of the expansive room where long vertical windows sit above ribbed concrete walls that run the perimeter of the building. These windows comprise the top half of the wall and are lined with narrow slats of redwood, referencing the bars of "a jail," yet the smaller rectangular windows above them suggest a sense of freedom. Like the glass doors below, which lead to the balconies and overlook the gardens, both sets of windows provide a glimpse of the surrounding nature. *All those years dancing in the auditorium during annual festivals and never once did I really notice those windows before.* In retrospect, I realize I looked without seeing.

Many kids start raging against their parents once they reach a certain age, and I was that child in spades — wild and unruly. Seasoned with adages like "children should be seen and not heard," "respect your elders," and "the nail that sticks out gets hammered in," I became a simmering pot waiting to boil. How I tortured my mother during those rebellious and headstrong years. My grandparents, aunties, and uncles acted as extended parents and reinforced certain ideas, such as narrowly defined roles of behaviour. For them Japanese women were supposed to be kind and gentle. Young girls were urged to be *yasashii*, not boisterous, noisy, or talkative, yet more often than not, my elders admonished me with an equally loud *yakamashii*!

Moving into adulthood, I began examining these notions with a more critical eye. Striking contrasts and dualities were called into question. I fiercely rejected and refused to comply with my family's outdated ways of thinking. Why should I remain silent and obedient? For all the positive Japanese attributes I openly embraced, the glaring inequities gnawed at my sense of self. At times I felt caged within those walls, confined in kimono, a token exotic on display and novelty act to entertain visitors. Trapped by the chains of tradition and a prisoner bound by beliefs, I often longed to be far away, free from the judgmental environment inherent within a monoculture and its rigid expectations of conformity. As a young woman of mixed race, I rejected patriarchy and had no interest in maintaining any status quo. The steep social hierarchy afforded me no place, except on the fringes of two different worlds. I resigned myself early on to the fact I would always be considered an outsider.

Have you ever wanted to take back words or undo certain events? I certainly do. During a drive to the Centre for dance practice one evening when I was thirteen or fourteen years of age, Mom reprimanded me for something or other. She didn't understand how I could be so disrespectful. Being a single parent, she must have felt she needed to be overly strict, controlling, and authoritative. But the more she dictated, the more I defied. Sitting in the back seat, I tried to tune out the sound of her voice and her ongoing tirade. Gazing out the window, I saw a reflection of my face burning red with anger. By the time we arrived at the Centre, I had grown increasingly restless and enraged. Those primary school years as a track-and-field sprinter had trained me for quick starts. Once the car doors swung open, in a flash I bolted from that parking lot, dashing up and over the grassy hills. In no time my stricken mother's shrill screams trailed off far behind me.

• • •

Attendees mill about the Noor Centre while Raymond Moriyama waits in the lobby for his ride. Like a celebrity, he's generous with his time, answering specific questions and obliging photo requests for those eager to snap a pose with the famed architect. He's taking a break before heading over to the opening of the exhibit "A Pride of Place: Building the First Japanese Canadian Cultural Centre" at the new JCCC, where he's the guest of honour.

My husband and I stop to say hello to Mr. Moriyama before leaving for the exhibit. Uncle George and Auntie Terry were long-time friends with the Moriyamas. Auntie Terry and Moriyama's wife, Sachi, knew each other from Vancouver, where they went to school together, and continued to be friends after both moved to Toronto.

At the Noor Cultural Centre's open house with Raymond Moriyama, September 22, 2019.

"I haven't seen your uncle George for a while. How's he doing? How's Terry?" Moriyama asks.

"They're OK. They've been very busy. They just moved from their apartment into a senior's home — not Momiji but another one on Sheppard."

"Oh, I'll have to give him a call."

"Yes, he'll be happy to hear from you."

Walking into the current JCCC, located conveniently around the corner on Garamond Court, we notice a photo display set up in the main hall includes a small-scale model of the

Wynford Drive building and artifacts detailing its history and
design. One of the glass cases holds a salvaged door handle and
in a moment of déjà vu, I'm spellbound at the level of attention
to detail.

. . .

When the old JCCC felt stretched for space in the 1970s,
discussions began and the idea of moving emerged as a possible solution. With the building unencumbered by debt and
mortgage-free by the 1980s, the board began a series of reviews
to weigh the difference in costs of renovation and building ver-
sus moving to a new location. Fundraising initiatives followed,
and in 1993 the board hired Moriyama Teshima Architects
to design a larger building on-site. Attempts to purchase the
neighbouring property and increase the lot size failed, but the
JCCC's building expansion committee persisted. The sheer
size of the Garamond Court commercial building, at about
114,000 square feet, featuring ample parking and discounted
pricing, attracted their attention. They put in a successful bid
and renovations soon followed.

. . .

How many countless barriers — real or imagined — do we
create for ourselves? By going back and surveying every room
of that landmark building on Wynford Drive, we've been able
to reexamine our own building blocks. We dredged up con-
tentious spirits and swept away the cobwebs of memory. In
examining every corner with fresh eyes, we're amazed at the
brilliant meshing of old and new — and filled with gratitude

for this rare opportunity to revisit the place where I spent so many of my formative years.

The gated entry, added after the JCCC sold the building, will no doubt be locked again after our departure. But now that they've been thrown open, will we close the doors of the past? Heading back to the car, we run into Mrs. Kanji and her daughter in the parking lot. We thank them for hosting this special event and welcoming us back on this historic day. Passing the stone monument, I point and share my secret. "Did you know there's a hidden space at the top of that sculpture?"

CHAPTER 8

ODORI PRIMER

"THE MAKEUP BRINGS you into the role. It's a time for you to step into that role and become the character," explains Ebizo Ichikawa. The third-generation performer is speaking through a translator to reporter Jon Wertheim on *60 Minutes*.[1] Ebizo, as he's known in Japan, is a kabuki superstar. Considered a blue blood of the stage, he's following in the steps of both his father and grandfather, and he honours this succession as his fated role. He's skilled at doing his own makeup, although dressing for the part often takes a few extra hands. In one production his costume weighed 130 pounds and needed to be packed with ice so he would remain cool throughout the performance.

This elaborate combination of song, theatre, mime, and dance is known as kabuki. Its origins date back to around 1603 and are credited to a shrine maiden named Izumo no Okuni.[2] To raise alms for her temple, Okuni took to the riverbanks in Kyoto, performing sacred songs and dances. Her innovative and colourful interpretations, which she called kabuki, soon attracted attention. Patrons flocked to the area to watch Okuni perform her signature dance style. Her renown spread and kabuki quickly gained in popularity. Many imitators followed, including performances in brothels, which led then shōgun Ieyasu Tokugawa to take a stand: women were forbidden from performing kabuki. To this day only men are permitted to perform it.

• • •

"Stop squirming; stand still." The voices are stern.

Standing in my underwear with arms extended straight out from my sides like a human scarecrow, I can't help but feel awkward and self-conscious. Impatiently, I wait to don that first layer — a long undershirt to contain my straw limbs — while worn hands adjust and smooth, tie and constrain. It's always a big production getting dressed in kimono. Anyone who's ever squeezed into a pair of Spanx knows how important the foundation of any outfit is. With kimono it's critical the base lies flat before adding the additional layers. Our performance days started early and ended late. Like Ebizo, we had generations of dancers in our family and a history of wearing kimono. Over the years Grandma amassed a fine selection of kimono and the accessories that accompany the traditional dress.

During the annual Obon summer festival held at Nathan Phillips Square in Toronto, we performed bon odori in the wide open square. There were no dressing rooms or stage area.

Instead, we'd speed through breakfast and take turns getting our hair and makeup done at home. Grandma, Bāchan, and Mom rushed to ready all us dancers for the big day. After generously slathering on baby powder to keep the sweat at bay, I'd find a corner in the living room of the Browning Avenue house and stand amongst the scattered boxes of kimono, slips, and obi. Age and size determined the pieces we wore: the first layer of under-kimono, or *nagajuban*, was either a long, sleeveless one-piece or two separates consisting of a full-length slip and a half-kimono undershirt with a stiff white collar. The kid-size slips and tops had sewn-on ties, while the adult ones were secured using narrow bands of fabric or stretchy elastic belts with Velcro fasteners.

During summertime festivals like Obon, brightly coloured cotton *yukata* are popular. Most of the children's *yukata* Grandma owned had the proper folds presewn into place to make dressing easier. Adult kimono tend to be one-size-fits-all. Depending on your height, the length needs to be adjusted to fit your body. In much the same way expert sewers know exactly where to pin the fabric, experienced dressers will easily fold and secure the kimono at just the right spot around the dancer's midsection.

All this underpinning is covered with a decorative obi, essentially a belt of long rigid fabric that is firmly rolled, wrapped, and knotted around the dancer's waist. After encircling the dancer, the stiff obi fabric is tied off at the back and the remaining length shaped into a bow. Centring a bow on a dancer's back is not easy. It takes skill and experience. Otherwise, the wearer struggles to remain standing while the tug and pull of alterations bounces them back and forth. Prefabricated versions, similar to clip-on bow ties, consisting of two pieces could be purchased: a short obi tied around the waist and a separate bow with a hook slipped into the band at the back. But these items were luxuries few possessed. These tight binding garments ensured our kimono remained neat throughout the long day until the actual performance and encouraged good posture even if we could barely breathe.

When we were young, our hair was too short to pull up into a bun. Acting as our hairdresser, Mom tried her best to add a bit of curl to our bone-straight bangs by manoeuvring a hot plug-in curling iron. Later, when my hair had grown, her scratchy paddle brush ripped through my scalp as she gathered my hair into one of her hands. And with a mouthful of long and short bobby pins held between her teeth, Mom carefully made a high ponytail. An aerosol can remained a fixture within arm's reach, ready to shower us with clouds of hairspray. With ponytail shellacked into place, the remaining length of hair was divided into sections to create a small bun and then pinned over to hide the elastic band with a million more stabbing bobby pins. Before a final choking of hairspray, I was instructed to shake my head to ensure the bun remained glued down in place. Delicate floral hair embellishments called *kanzashi* added a final decorative touch. Positioned on an angle at the edge of the bun, they were the last of the piercing needles to be embedded in my skull.

· · ·

Tsuki ga deta deta, tsuki ga deta, a yoi yoi ...

From a distance the sound of Kunio's melodic singing rises to the quiet of the third floor. His voice carries and gradually becomes louder, accompanied by the rhythm of his footsteps bouncing off the concrete walls in the JCCC stairwell. As he climbs the stairs, the scuffling of shoes against hard concrete announces his arrival. He stops in the main office across the hall before wandering into the meeting room where I'm sitting. The neighbour, family friend, and community elder I once knew as Mr. Suyama has taken on an additional role as my boss during my time as JCCC newsletter editor from 1987 to 1993. Eyes on the computer, I'm focused on typing articles for the next edition. Before I have time to look up, he places beside me a small Styrofoam plate filled with an assortment of sushi freshly prepared by the army of volunteers during Centre events.

"Here."

I barely have a moment to say thank you before he's out the door again, humming the melody and breaking back into song where he left off, "*sano yoi yoi …*"

His voice trails off, as if someone has their hand on the volume, growing fainter and muffled as he walks toward his office on the other side of the building. Strolling along with his characteristic unhurried elegance, Mr. Suyama's standard work uniform consisted of a dark-coloured suit, white shirt, and understated tie. But on special occasions and festivals, he was one of the few men who regularly dressed in kimono.

Born in Cumberland, British Columbia, on Christmas Eve in 1927, Kunio was the fifth child in a family of ten children. During the war the Suyama family was sent to Lemon Creek. Perhaps it was there a teenage Kunio glimpsed his future as an MC when he hosted a special school concert in 1946. Later that year the Suyama family were shipped off to Japan, although Kunio's brother Toke and a sister decided to remain behind in Canada. The Suyamas' eldest son had been studying in Japan before the war began and wrote to warn his family to remain in Canada, but that fateful letter never arrived. Conditions in Japan were difficult. Fortunately, they had family in Uruzu, Fukuoka-ken, a farming community where they settled. Located on the main island of Kyūshū, Grandmother Suyama's home was near Tsuiki Airbase, which at the time was held by the Americans. Bilingual Kunio found work as an interpreter for the U.S. Army in Kokura City.

Within a few years, he had saved up enough money to return to Canada and arrived in October 1950 with two of his sisters. Kunio married Yoshiye Omori in 1955; the couple later settled in Toronto on Browning Avenue and raised three children (Debbie, Julie, and Larry). Their house sat on the corner in between our place and my grandparents' home. Whenever we passed by, we'd always stop to say hi. Of the handful of Japanese families who lived in the area, we knew every one of them.

Like our family, many JCs remained rooted to the area, while the majority of our Greek neighbours left during the gentrification of the Danforth and surrounding vicinity. Reported to be one of the first JC members of Toronto's ACTRA (Alliance of Canadian Cinema, Television and Radio Artists) in the early 1960s, Kunio was recognized for his work in commercials and television dramas. The actor and amateur singer also enjoyed working on stage in Japanese plays and concerts. He had already become established in the community as a board member for many organizations by the time he became the executive director at the JCCC, a position he held from 1986 to 1997. His smiling face and warm demeanour made him a natural community ambassador. From Obon to Caravan and other community events, the ever-present MC must have greeted thousands of people.

• • •

While the details of those early years in the 1970s are a bit fuzzy, bon odori sparked the beginning of my Japanese dance lessons. After the Second World War, bon odori found new audiences in Toronto and the venues were many: Christie Pits, Dufferin Park, Nathan Phillips Square, Mel Lastman Square, North York Civic Centre, and finally, the JCCC. Year after year spectators grew accustomed to watching minyō performances during Obon. In my mind it seemed we dancers cycled through the same numbers over and over again, although to be fair, there were some updated and contemporary versions added over time.

While the names of the dances escape me now, some of the most memorable ones used props: semicircular hats made of woven straw had slim strips of fabric that knotted around the chin; long, red, cotton fingerless gloves tied above the wrist and looped onto one finger; a black-and-white polka dot scarf resembled a small towel. And then there were dances where we used percussion instruments called *kachi-kachi*. All the kids used tiny circular finger castanets made from two wooden discs. Fastened together with black elastic and topped with little silver jingle bells, these *kachi-kachi* were lacquered in bright high-gloss colours: cobalt blue on one side and poppy red on the other. Our cute clackers were a far cry from the elegant adult versions the older women used. Both types created a clicking sound when struck together, but the latter were made from red-lacquered rectangular slats of wood tied with red fine silk cord and finished with tassels. We knew we were no longer children when our teacher insisted we forgo the minis and use the long ones.

To this day, every year in early spring, the TBC puts an ad calling for volunteers in all the local community papers and newsletters. Everyone is welcome to participate in the bon odori with the TBC Minyō Group. Formed in the early 1950s, the group's focus is on teaching folk dances. Practices begin in mid-April in anticipation of their main performance at Obon. Other dance clubs like the Buyō Group, Sakura Kai, and the Haru-Yagi Kai rehearsed the traditional folk dances separately but joined together with the TBC group to perform en masse in the heat of summer. There were many familiar faces when everyone came together during Obon. It didn't matter if we knew their names or which club they belonged to. We were all there to dance.

The Buyō Group, the TBC's other troupe of dancers, has been led by Sensui Kozakura since 1994. It performs in the modern *shin-buyō* style of Japanese dance, with a repertoire ranging from classical and folk styles to contemporary ones using popular music. One important aspect of the group's lessons is *kitsuke*, known as the proper wearing of a kimono. As a pioneer in dance, the Sakura Kai had a lengthy community history. It was founded in the 1960s by Masae Shiozaki, Chiyo Seko, and Irene Tsujimoto, women who wanted to ensure *buyō*, as one of the oldest cultural traditions from Japan, was not forgotten in Canada and passed on to future generations. Like the Sansei Choir, the Sakura Kai preceded the JCCC and performed at the Nationbuilders events at the CNE. Its traditional folk and semiclassical dances are influenced by the *Fujima-ryū* style.

Following in the footsteps of generations past, young girls in the JC community were enrolled in Japanese dance lessons. Our family has always been a bit more traditional. Perhaps it was due to Bāchan's influence as our earlier matriarch and Grandma, who often said we were raised with the old-fashioned ways from Japan. The women in our family joined the Haru-Yagi Kai, a dance group founded by my great-aunt Harumi Nakamura. This was the same troupe Auntie Norma used to dance with and included former members from the Sansei Choir and Dancers, the youth choir Auntie Marlene belonged to. By the time I became a member in the late 1970s, Auntie Norma, who is ten years my senior, had already left Haru-Yagi Kai.

At first Chiyo Seko provided dance instruction for the Sansei Choir and Dancers while juggling other responsibilities. Auntie Harumi stepped in to assist and took the lead in 1967. When the choir disbanded in 1974, Auntie Harumi organized a new troupe from those students who wanted to continue dancing. Haru-Yagi Kai became one of the main schools for Japanese classical dance and strove to impart proper form and posture as the basis of good classical dance skills. Affiliated with the JCCC, the club performed at the Centre and other venues. Harumi's elegance as a dancer had few equals. Like a seasoned pro, she demonstrated specific steps with effortless grace. Her youngest daughter, Sanae, followed in her footsteps for a time, assisting her with our instruction after receiving teaching papers from the *Wakayagi-ryū* school in Chicago.

Born Harumi Tomotsugu in 1924 on Cortes Island in British Columbia, Auntie Harumi found herself en route to Japan before her second birthday. Like many families at the time, her mother, Kikuno Tomotsugu, wanted her children to be educated in Japan and journeyed there with the intention of leaving her three kids with an uncle in Okayama-ken while they attended school. On the way there, young Harumi became ill and, instead of leaving the child, her mother decided to bring Harumi with her when she returned home. During the two-week ship voyage back to Canada, Mrs. Tomotsugu befriended a Japanese man named Masao Nakashima, who suffered terrible seasickness. She helped care for the sick passenger, and this marked the beginning of a lifelong friendship between the two families.

From Cortes Island, the Tomotsugus moved to Stave Falls, near Mission, British Columbia, where Harumi's father, Yoshigoro, continued to work in the forestry industry for the Stave Lake Cedar Co. Her mother cooked for the men staying at the forestry camp. Yoshigoro Tomotsugu belonged to the generation who thought girls could forgo school and needed to learn how to cook and sew, but his wife pressed for a proper education. Around 1930 after Harumi turned five, Mrs. Tomotsugu arranged for a short-term stay with the well-to-do and educated Yamashita family in Vancouver. Businessman Shintaro Yamashita owned two businesses on Gore Avenue near the corner of Powell Street: Yama Taxi and an electric appliance store called Yama Radio. He was the eldest brother of Masao Nakashima,[3] the man Mrs. Tomotsugu helped on the ship. Shintaro's wife, Yoshiko, played the koto and was a certified *Seiha-ryū* instructor of the stringed instrument. She continued the koto practice in Canada by providing lessons to many students, including her own children. "There's nothing for Harumi in the woods," they said. "Let her stay with us."

Young Harumi did not speak any English when she arrived in the busy city, and the Yamashitas soon became like family. The Yamashita's five children included a daughter named Terry (Teruye), who was about five years younger than Harumi. In retrospect it seems incredibly generous to take in strangers, but the family may have felt obligated to repay the debt of kindness shown to their brother. Mrs. Tomotsugu found a place

JAPANESE DANCERS
—1939—

Auntie Harumi (far left) and Auntie Terry (far right) demonstrate their dancing skills in Vancouver.

around the corner from the Yamashitas and settled on Powell Street. She continued to help Mrs. Yamashita with her busy household over the years. During the late 1930s, Harumi's two older brothers finished school and returned from Japan, joining their mother and sister in Vancouver. Both found work at the British Columbia Pulp and Paper Co. in Woodfibre. Though Mr. Tomotsugu continued to work in Stave Falls, he often took the train to visit his family. He eventually decided to retire from logging and worked at Yama Taxi once he joined his family in Vancouver.

Harumi and Terry grew up together, attending Japanese music and odori lessons with Tonogai sensei, a *Wakayagi buyō* teacher. Harumi was in her second year at Fairview High School of Commerce in December 1941 when Canada declared war on Japan, and she was forced to leave. In 1942 Harumi's family faced another separation: Yoshigoro was relocated to Monte Lake near Kamloops; his sons were sent to a road camp in Schreiber, Ontario; and his wife and daughter were incarcerated with the Yamashitas in Minto City, British Columbia. After the war and mandatory relocation, Harumi's brothers secured farm work in Chatham, Ontario, where the Tomotsugu family reunited in 1945. By June 1946 Harumi had met and then lost her first husband, Seichi Ohashi, when he accidentally fell off a bridge and drowned a mere month after they were married. Though Harumi died in 2012, it was years later when I heard this tragic story.

The Nakamura clan lived and worked on a farm nearby just outside of Chatham. My grandfather's younger brother Gord was friends with Harumi's brothers, and it wasn't long before the two met. When my grandfather found work in Toronto in 1947, the rest of the family followed. Despite the cap on how many Japanese were allowed to relocate to Toronto, Harumi managed to sneak in with one of her brothers two years later. Harumi and Gord reunited. They married in 1951 and had five children. Along the way they both made significant contributions to the JC community: Uncle Gordie, as we called him, was a JCCC board member for two terms from 1971 to 1973, and Auntie Harumi taught odori to scores of young JCs, including her own daughters, during more than fifteen years of volunteer service presiding over the Haru-Yagi Kai club. She retired in 1984. During that entire time, Uncle Gordie tirelessly chauffeured her and other relatives across the city without complaint.

In the days of their early courtship, Harumi invited her long-time friend Terry Yamashita to meet Gord's mother and siblings in the Nakamura home on Duchess Street in Toronto. There Terry met my grandfather's youngest brother, George. In another twist of fate, the two later married, and Terry and Harumi became officially related as sisters-in-law within the ever-growing Nakamura clan.

• • •

There's something very calming about austere and unembellished surroundings. Nothing to compete for attention or draw the eye. The JCCC on Wynford Drive was built like a bomb shelter with its massive concrete-block walls and minimalist, almost institutional, but nevertheless Japanese-inspired aesthetic. If there ever is an architectural study in brutalism, it certainly deserves a chapter. Within those walls I began attending weekly Japanese classical dance classes. My less-than-perfect skills and earlier folk training were soon to be expanded on and refined under the stern tutelage of Auntie Harumi. It happened by chance.

Growing up I was more of a tomboy. When I was about seven years old and Dee nine, Mom thought we needed more discipline in our lives and decided to introduce us to judo. About a year and a programming switch later, our evening judo classes coincided with odori practice. In the old JCCC, there were only a handful of rooms on the lower level, and with other evening classes taking place, I quickly ran into some of my cousins as well as one of my neighbourhood friends. Discovering they were part of the Haru-Yagi Kai provided enough enticement to swap one set of lessons for the other. And since our relative Harumi Nakamura headed the group, I'm sure my mom felt some peace of mind knowing her young girls were spending time with family and friends. Dee never felt welcome among the dancers. Shortly after she switched back to sparring with the judo guys until joint pain intervened and she had to quit.

Handed down from one generation of teachers to the next, the classical and folk dances we learned told a story. Dancers were divided into small groups according to age, height, and skill level and were taught a classical number to be performed on stage. The more advanced dancers performed in several numbers, while the youngest kids did only one. Each week's lesson doubled as a rehearsal in preparation for the next event. And similar to other stage productions, each dance number had specific costumes, accessories, and props, which became more sophisticated as our troupe grew larger and had more resources.

The favoured dancers were always selected to perform the most beautiful dances and wore elaborately decorated silk kimono with extra-long sleeves and padded hemlines, elaborate updos, and special headpieces. My group, comprised of the few mixed dancers like me, were assigned what we called the man dances, where we marched around with big, forceful movements and pretended to wield swords in some type of samurai drama. For costumes we wore the typical men's outfit: a plain cotton kimono tucked into dark wide-leg pants called *hakama*. The props might include a fan or straw hat, and our hair was styled into a simple ponytail or topknot.

Aunt Harumi's sombre demeanour and exacting eye instilled fear and respect. Laughing and other childish antics were frowned upon. We were expected to take a serious approach at practice. If we ever complained about our great-aunt's strict ways, Mom shrugged it off. Harumi wasn't strict, she'd argue. Back in Mom's dancing days, she had an odori teacher who relished in correcting bad posture with a quick knee to the centre of the back while wrenching shoulders into their proper position. Other times the sensei would make a forceful adjustment by suddenly pressing behind a dancer's knees with her own to ensure they were bent at the proper angle.

A cherished photo of my former dance group was taken in the JCCC auditorium as we performed on stage. The task was to present ourselves in a unified manner, moving together as a fluid whole in sync with every gesture. Somehow the camera managed to capture each dancer in a completely different position. A snapshot in time that never fails to coax a smile.

On performance days we'd wait until the last moment to get dressed in our costumes, lounging around in our under-kimono with our zori and white tabi. Over time we learned to get into these garments on our own. Although I've never taken to flip-flops, wearing zori is different. The dress versions have solid wedge soles and are covered in decorative material. Tabi are made of stiff cotton with a padded bottom and are similar in shape to short ankle socks, but they separate the large toe into a section away from the other toes. There's no shortage of Western-style socks mimicking tabi with their stretchy pull-on fabric like regular socks. Tabi mimic old-fashioned spats to a degree, but instead of button-up sides, they feature metal-like triangular tabs on one side of the ankle that disappear when hooked through a string on the other side and create a straight seam when closed.

One benefit of being part of a club was having a skilled hair and makeup person. She ensured our consistency in look: lots of blush swept up onto the temples and special red lipstick from Japan dispensed from a foil-covered tube. Club dressers

Dancing "Harusame" during Caravan 1980.

helped us with our costumes before and after the stage program when we changed into our matching club kimono for the folk dancing portion of the show. These women were the mothers of current or former dancers who knew the proper dressing protocols and voluntarily shared their folding and binding skills.

The Haru-Yagi Kai dance club's regular performance circuit included annual JCCC festivals such as Haru Matsuri and major events like the citywide Festival Caravan when the Centre transformed itself into the Tokyo pavilion. Both the Haru-Yagi Kai and Sakura Kai dance groups had classical and folk elements to their shows. Different days and times were allotted, and each club presented select classical dances on stage inside the auditorium as well as the ensemble pieces that included the entire troupe. Both groups also learned an array of *minyō* or folk dances to be performed outside, weather permitting.

Minyō became an attraction at Caravan. On warm summer evenings, we'd head outside and dance on the soft grass. Dancers ordered by height, from shortest to tallest, assembled into a circle before the music began. Other times we'd make our entrance from different directions of intersecting lines that closed to form the circle. Adding to the ambiance, servers wearing happi coats welcomed visitors in the adjacent beer garden decorated with hanging paper lanterns and infused with the intoxicating aromas of grilled chicken teriyaki and deep-fried tempura. Whether people flocked to the Centre for the festive environment, delicious Japanese food, or cold drinks, patrons enjoyed live entertainment from that choice vantage point. Others sat on the grassy slopes to watch the dancers and listen to Japanese folk music accompanied by taiko drummers.

As the big event approached, it was a mad rush to get things right. Many extra rehearsals were scheduled up to the last minute. For a few nights a week, we'd learn all the old and sometimes new *minyō*. Barbara Nikaido was an equally no-nonsense and demanding instructor who specialized in the *minyō* portion of the performances. Florist by day and *minyō* teacher by night, she held practices in the back of her flower shop on Greenwood Avenue, where a group of us dancers gathered and painstakingly ran through the numbers. An authoritative Nikaido marched up and down the lines of dancers, cigarette dangling from her lips. Shouting over the music, she issued corrections or pointers, never missing a beat while clapping her hands to the rhythms. On performance days two very different teachers stood on the sidelines. Both tried to remain inconspicuous as they quietly gestured to passing *minyō* dancers to smile and look cheerful for the gathered onlookers.

• • •

One day before class, my grade ten English teacher asked to see me.

"Most of the class failed," he started in his soft-spoken voice. "But you managed to grasp what I was looking for and, in fact, did quite well."

"Really?" I responded.

He was referring to the test on John Wyndham's sci-fi thriller *The Chrysalids*. The book is set in an intolerant futuristic society in which those who deviate from the norm are cast out and banished to the wild country by the larger community. Unfortunately, in this post–nuclear war environment, mutations in plants and animals are more commonplace than most liked to believe.

"Did they read the book? It was pretty straightforward," I said.

He paused, shrugging. "I just wanted to let you know. I hope you'll keep going with your studies. You know, I think you really have something here … and not to give up."

Looking back I recognize the outsider theme in the book resonated with me. I understood what it meant to be an outcast, an alien — it was something I was already familiar with.

Midway through grade ten, I started working as an extra in a film and figured I might as well drop out of school. Despite being enrolled in enriched level courses, I was still passing with less than 50 percent attendance. School was boring. There were so many other exciting things I could be doing with my time. Mom eventually gave up trying to wake me every morning and, instead of fighting with me to get ready for school, left me to sleep in.

I managed to find a talent agent, who sent me to model and commercial auditions, but her enthusiasm waned when I failed to produce more than a bit part here and there. It was so discouraging to be passed over time and time again. Sure, I was always one of the first ones to be noticed during casting, but it never went anywhere. Directors wanted a token Asian or someone white. I wasn't Japanese enough to be picked for Asian roles and not fully white to land those roles either. And no one was looking for a mixed race character. My hopes of launching into an acting career fizzled with the awareness there weren't any parts for me to play.

I was about to leave another fruitless audition when one of the agents suddenly offered some unsolicited advice: "You know, I just thought of the perfect role for you … I think you'd make a great alien." He exchanged glances with his partner. Both of them began nodding as they stared at me. "Yeah, I can see it, you'd be perfect … not that we're doing any sci-fi stuff now, but something to keep in mind for the future. You'd be the perfect alien."

As an aspiring young actor, it wasn't what I wanted to hear.

• • •

If Japan seems behind the times with its male-dominated kabuki, we're hardly further ahead in North America. As it is, lead roles for Asians are few and far between, so when these roles do arise, it seems shameful that preference continues to be given to white actors. Audiences worldwide were outraged when films like *Aloha*, *Ghost in the Shell*, and *Doctor Strange* cast white actors to play parts that were actually written as Asian or biracial characters. For Asian actors tired of being upstaged by white people, it served as a sad reminder and demonstrated how common whitewashing practices still are in Hollywood.

Classic stage productions like *The Mikado*, *Miss Saigon*, and *The Nutcracker* have a long history of whitewashing. Essentially, it is the modern-day equivalent of yellowface, a common practice in opera, theatre, and ballet dating back to the seventeenth century that managed to sidestep its way into film and television.[4] Similar to the offensive practice of blackface, yellowface provides a caricature of Asian characters where actors don makeup or prosthetics to play the evil villain or an exotic enchantress or to provide comic relief.

Wealthy American and European consumers were already familiar with Chinese decorative objects and decor, called chinoiserie, when the opera *The Mikado* debuted in 1885. The successful production created a huge demand for Japanese merchandise, or japonaiserie, and became famous for introducing the idea of impersonating Japanese people by using objects, music, and scenes to transport audiences to an exotic and mysterious fantasyland. White stage performers used standard exaggerated racial gestures to add to the comic effect, a "form of racial performance" that "eroded the responsibility to represent Japanese people or culture in factual ways."[5]

Despite criticism and protests throughout the decades that followed, discussions regarding *The Mikado* often focus on free expression and ignore the problems of how inaccurate portrayals far removed from reality sexually exoticize and objectify Japanese culture and people: "The libidinal desires inherent in *The Mikado*'s brand of yellowface emphasize Japaneseness as deeply foreign and its attractions as those of the alien: novelty, mystery, strangeness, and difference."[6] Rather than providing accurate or realistic cultural representations, this othering technique favoured by many theatrical productions repeatedly depicted Japanese as aliens and reinforced racial prejudices.

U.S. media and advertisers also utilized yellowface as a powerful means to reinforce and propagate anti-Asian ideology and enabled hurtful stereotypes to be perpetuated within mainstream society.[7] For audiences who might never have had the opportunity to meet actual Asians, white actors employed their inherent privilege to define them and other groups.

In the world of ballet, Toronto alderman Ying Hope issued a formal complaint in 1981 to the Ontario Human Rights Commission after attending a National Ballet of Canada performance of *The Nutcracker* that included an offensive Chinese dance intended as comic relief. Hope called the scene where one man spanked another with a parasol shocking. He went on to describe how their outmoded costumes, Fu Manchu moustaches, and exaggerated gaits were inaccurate stereotypes. Not only did he claim it was racist, but he also feared the children in the audience might be influenced to think this was typical Chinese behaviour.[8] His protest created a series of commentaries in local newspapers, but many people were dismissive of his concerns and the production continued until it was completely revamped in 1995.

The fight against yellowface resurfaced in 2017 as others stepped in with new efforts to eliminate these hurtful parodies. Ballet soloist Georgina Pazcoquin and Phil Chan, an arts administrator and educator, began the Final Bow for Yellowface[9] movement by pledging their love of the art form. They acknowledged that to achieve actual diversity, they were committed to eliminating yellowface on stage. The group continues to encourage people to share their experiences and invites anyone to sign the online pledge on their yellowface.org website.

Scores of film actors, such as John Wayne, Peter Sellers, Marlon Brando, Mickey Rooney, and Katherine Hepburn, have made lucrative careers in yellowface throughout the decades. In 1930 a set of moral guidelines called the Motion Picture Production Code (a.k.a. the Hays Code[10]) was introduced. Enforced until 1968, these guidelines were initially advisory, but they later required mandatory script reviews and covered every aspect of onscreen behaviour. In this respect the Hays Code essentially became a convenient type of film censorship that limited options for racialized and ethnic actors. For example, one rule barred miscegenation: any onscreen depiction of romantic encounters between actors of different races or the suggestion of interracial unions was strictly prohibited. Yellowface, in effect, became a way of bending these rules.

Actors continue to speak out on issues of race and representation within the film industry. The hashtags #OscarsSoWhite and #WhiteWashedOut surfaced in 2015, unleashing waves of backlash against Hollywood's continued use of white actors in leading roles with little to no representation of other ethnic groups. Rare lead roles for Asians continue to be filled by or rewritten for white actors. Although every new action movie by Keanu Reeves, Jackie Chan, and Dwayne Johnson reminds audiences we exist, for the most part, Asians remain invisible or continue to be depicted as the foreigner or hypersexualized exotic.

To combat this, the Annenberg Inclusion Initiative endeavours to take a critical look at films and specifically examine onscreen representation. Based out of the University of Southern California, the group reported Hollywood rarely includes Asians and Pacific Islanders in lead roles. In assessing films released between 2007 and 2019, researchers determined stereotypes and underrepresentation may be contributing factors to U.S.-based incidents of harassment and violence against Asians.[11]

Kim's Convenience, a Canadian TV show about a Korean family celebrated for its Asian cast, was cancelled despite successful ratings. A spinoff from the series followed, but it featured the only non-Asian character from the show. In a *Toronto Star*[12] article, a former cast member spoke out about ignored opportunities and disparities behind the scenes, including being paid less than the non-Asian actors, and failing to consult with the Asian cast or utilize their experiences for any of the show's story content. This didn't surprise me. Back when I started working at Citytv in 1989, the local TV channel attracted scores of multicultural fans who found their communities represented in the diversity of on-air personalities. Though behind this facade, white men ran the show.

It's not all bad news though. In 2018 *Crazy Rich Asians* showed Hollywood that a film featuring Asian actors in lead roles could become a blockbuster. On the heels of that success, many Asian actors and directors secured a historic number of first-time Oscar nominations and wins. While the cast and crew of films like *Parasite* (2019) and *Minari* (2020) may not be household names in North America yet, their recognition by the larger film community may pave the way for others. Sometimes it just takes one actor, film, or TV program to inspire a new generation who feel validated when they see their own stories depicted on screen.

Isn't it time we looked for collective solutions instead of elevating one culture above all others or ranking ethnicities from inferior to superior? Perhaps I'm an idealist with grand hopes, but I envision a place in the not too distant future where Asians are celebrated and not defined as the demeaning punchline to someone else's crude joke or repeatedly cast as the despised downtrodden, lethal assassin, or alien. We are multidimensional individuals with our own complexities, nuances, contradictions, and depth of character. We, too, can be the hero of the story, one who triumphs over adversity against all odds.

CHAPTER 9

MISS TOKYO

"YOU NEVER SAW such an ugly baby. Eww." My father pauses for dramatic effect before launching into his favourite story.

"There's all these babies in the nursery so I ask the nurse to point out which one is mine. And when she does, I say, 'Nooo.'" He shakes his head in disbelief. "'You've gotta be kidding! There's no way that's my kid,' I said to her. There had to be some mistake. I couldn't believe it. I refused to take her home from the hospital. I said, 'Nope, no way!'" His eyes darken as he reflects and adds, "But her mother made me." He stops again and, glancing in my direction, a proud smile suddenly lights up his face. "Now just look at her."

While my father never lost his German accent, I learned to tune out his gruff, guttural voice. He relished telling his ugly duckling tale but hearing him repeat it over and over again disgusted me. As the reviled subject, I stopped listening years ago. In fact, as soon as I detect him starting up, I turn away and look for something, anything, to absorb my attention.

My sister, Dee, had been such a beautiful baby. Like most first-born children, she had entire photo albums dedicated to recording every moment of her life, at least for the two-and-a-half years before I was born. From the handful of baby pictures of me that exist, I have to agree I was a funny-looking baby: slits where eyes should have been, ghostly white skin topped with a tuft of auburn hair. On my Japanese side, my grandmother's sister had her own hairdressing salon, and whenever I visited my great-aunt as a kid, she decided I looked best with a close-cropped pixie cut. Perhaps she thought it suited me and my tomboyish ways. Being mistaken for a young boy allowed me to fly under the radar. Running amok with neighbourhood friends, I remained free from the pressures of staying neat and clean or sitting still in pretty dresses.

Initially, my father's narrative focused solely on my unfortunate outward appearance. I was his little *Schwächling* then, as he liked to call me, my German nickname for "weakling." He'd pinch my biceps and wonder aloud, "How could this child, my own offspring, be so ugly, so puny, a little weakling?" Brainwashed from an early age by the wartime propaganda of his day, my father viewed the world through a distorted lens. In his mind he believed he was a perfect specimen superior to others — a representation of Aryan standards with his sharp intellect, unmatched physicality, strawberry blond hair, and blue eyes. Everything I was not and would never be. He prided himself on his physical prowess, boasting how fit and handsome he'd been in his prime and how, by moving to Canada, he missed his chance to play professionally for Germany's national soccer team. As age set in, he remained his biggest fan.

At some point, I'm not sure when, he determined I had magically transformed. Growing out of my awkward stage, I had become acceptable in his eyes — good-looking even. This development provided him with the opportune twist to his fable's progression, which he now told with greater relentlessness. Like scar tissue, in a mask of false strength, my skin grew thick. Away from my father's critical gaze, I evolved into a fierce teenager — reckless and defiant. During those welcome reprieves when he remained absent from our lives, his tale lost its power to torment me. Instead, it had the opposite effect: it inspired a seething contempt. No longer a small child who feared him, I did not care if I had his approval, nor did I ever seek it. Gradually over the years, my anger toward him subsided. Though I never condoned my father's erratic behaviour or racist and misogynistic rantings, I came to realize he is a product of his environment. I think my mother tried to see the best in him, but years of disappointment led to their separation. Each time he dismissed her hopes and dreams for the future, it slowly peeled away his veneer of promise and potential.

Fast forward to one of my father's infrequent visits. Never one for gifts, he usually made a point of being scarce around Christmas. One year he decided to take us clothes shopping. Since he never bothered to pay child support, Mom might have suggested he treat us kids. Dee recalls needing a winter coat, or maybe we caught him on a day when he happened to be in a particularly generous mood. Whatever the circumstances, all of us remember, it was the first and only time we went shopping with my father. Though I can't recall the name of the mall or stores we visited, Dee likely suggested we visit some of the fine European boutiques she knew well from her shopping exploits.

It was during the 1980s, in the height of my teenage punk rocker stage, but I still managed to find a couple of outfits I absolutely loved. At first I thought I had to choose between the expensive items: two beautiful black suits — one had pants and a blazer and the other a knit sweater with a matching skirt. My father surprised me by saying I could get them both, and without hesitating, he pulled out a huge wad of bills and settled the account. In those earlier days, my father was always flush with cash. Despite his frugal approach to fatherhood, his business making precision sheet metal parts provided him with a substantial income and allowed him to make a fortune, though he later squandered it.

It's Christmas Day. Dressed for the holiday season in my new finery and infused with attitude, I sauntered down Browning Avenue to my Japanese grandparents' home. Family gatherings were normally characterized by loud and animated chatter. Strutting in — clad head to toe in black — a hush greeted me. The room fell silent as heads strained to look and gawking eyes surveyed my outfit: a black pleather suit, heavy black eyeliner, black lipstick, black nail polish. Grandpa suddenly jumped up from his chair and, breaking the silence, blurted out, "Oh! Must take picture, get camera." He scurried past me as I stood in the hallway. Excited by this photo opportunity, the amateur photographer quickly reappeared with his prized 35 mm Canon camera and launched into a photo shoot.

My dramatic entrance that day is one of those images forever captured in time. Seared into the memories of everyone in attendance and even those who weren't, it's become part of our family lore. To this day no one will ever let me forget that

Sweet sixteen? Pleather-loving teen in the early 1980s.

moment. Thankfully, this ongoing needling fails to administer its intended sting of embarrassment. Instead of being provoked, as the black sheep of the family, I embraced the ugly long ago. Even at Grandpa's funeral, in a tribute from the grandchildren, my cousin Bryan couldn't resist mentioning that day. Prior to the service all the grandkids gathered to compile some words of remembrance. Dee, as the oldest, was expected to speak but refused, afraid of being overcome with emotion, and the responsibility fell to me. While I spoke of how Grandpa accepted all of us as unique individuals and never questioned or judged, Bryan was quick to remind the gathered mourners of my punk rock stage and how Grandpa "made light of the situation and everyone had a good laugh" at my expense.

• • •

The text time-stamp reads: Nov 4, 2017, 6:38 PM:

> Camille: BTW shaved my head don't freak out.
>   Also, when do you need to be picked up?
> Suzanne: OK can't wait to see you. (I add a
>   bowling ball emoji.)
>   Should be done after 8.
> Camille: Okay, meet you in the usual spot.

After a long day working at the annual Whole Life Expo, an alternative health show staged by my employer, *Vitality* magazine, I step outside into the November evening air. A cold, damp wind slaps my face. It's threatening rain, so I head back into the Metro Toronto Convention Centre to wait for my ride, not sure what to expect as the silver Jeep pulls up on Front

Street. Rushing out to our vehicle, I notice a reflection from the overhead streetlights — a shaved head glows in the backseat. Within a few days, a slight stubble has formed on Camille's head; a soft peach fuzz where thick, luxurious locks once hung. I'm inspired. *Just like Grandpa*, I smile to myself.

"Let's get some glamour shots!" I say as I position Camille in front of the sunroom's garden doors. With our dark-brown velvet blackout curtains serving as a backdrop, Camille's large, blue eyes pop as if magnified in the closely cropped headshots. "Who wore it better — you or Sinéad?" I ask. I've tried to capture the look from the Irish singer's video for the hit song "Nothing Compares 2 U." Though O'Connor enjoyed huge popularity during my youth, I'm met with a blank stare.

"I'm not familiar with who that is."

Later, I proudly post the photo on Facebook with the caption "My beautiful baby — turns 20 today! Where did the time go?"

Camille's face radiates with beauty. Shocked relatives remarked they were amazed Camille had the guts to go hairless. It wouldn't be the last time Camille decided to sport a shaved head. Later I cautioned against it — thinking it gave the appearance of a cancer survivor. I've known several women who lost all their hair due to chemotherapy, but none of them dared to be seen in public with a bald head. Whether out of embarrassment, insecurity, or vanity, they felt the need to wear a wig, scarf, or hat.

Funny how no one bats an eyelash when a man shaves his head or goes bald naturally. Men are often encouraged to shear what's left of their locks when they start to lose their hair. Who sets these standards? The onus is always upon women to look presentable and to make the effort for the sake of others. Even if we pride ourselves on our individuality, intellect, or societal contributions, we're still influenced by what we see when we look in the mirror. In *The Face: A Time Code*, Ruth Ozeki questions the pressures women feel to look attractive: "As a Zen priest, I probably shouldn't be using makeup at all. Isn't there a precept against lipstick? If not, shouldn't there be? Surely I should be a bit less attached to my physical appearance by now, no? Is my lingering attachment a barometer of my unenlightened state? The author in me is apparently still vain. She is still trying. Is there a time when a woman is officially old enough to stop caring?"[1]

Throughout Japan's history, a woman's hairstyle symbolized her marital status, social class, religion, and age. Historically, upper-class Japanese women had servants to help tend to their long hair, while lower classes leaned toward shorter and easier-to-maintain hair styles. Women considered their hair to be one of their main features and strove to mirror the beauty ideals of their day. The *Encyclopedia of Hair*[2] by Victoria Sherrow has a chapter on Japanese trends that details how long black hair, preferably waist length, was considered ideal; anything shorter was thought of as an affliction. And regardless of any other physical features, if a woman had long, thick, and shiny hair, she was deemed attractive.

To shave a woman's head usually signified two different things: the ritual Buddhist priests and nuns perform before entering spiritual life or a punishment marking a woman who had committed a crime. In the Middle Ages, many people followed superstitions related to hair. Even to this day, many Japanese fear they will attract bad luck if they wash their hair on New Year's Day and schedule haircuts prior to the holiday to ensure good luck. During the Meiji period, women were required to follow strict rules governing the appearance of their hair for the sake of maintaining the status quo in their male-dominated society. Sherrow explains how one law stipulated permission be granted by husbands or fathers before a woman was allowed to cut her hair. Another law, passed in 1872, banned short hair on women as these hairstyles were considered radical and not in keeping with Japanese traditions.[3]

On learning this, I'm happy to maintain my enduring preference for short hair. As a Zen priest, Ruth Ozeki shaved her head as part of the ordination ceremony: "Head-shaving is a symbolic act of renunciation and cutting one's ties with the secular world. The act felt extreme, definitive and transformative.... As Soto Zen practitioners, we'd appropriated this ritual, along with other ceremonial Zen forms, from Japan, but wasn't that just another example of Oriental exoticism? Surely the ritual of head-shaving is maladapted to our western cultural context where, historically it has meant something very different. In the past, shaving a woman's head was a form of public shaming."[4]

• • •

I am neither quiet nor demure — *yakamashii*, not *yasashii*. I'm too restless to sit still or hold my tongue. Like my Japanese grandfather and German father, I've always believed language should be spoken plainly and to the point. Years of working in television taught me to be brief, if not blunt. I never got the hang of this "inside and outside face" prevalent in the JC community. My straightforward and stubborn character made it difficult for me to maintain different personas: one for inside the home with family and close friends and another one for outside in public.

My non-Asian work colleagues might say they found me too serious, overly formal, cold even. I had grown used to roaming, moving around in different circles. I never liked saying goodbye, so I never really said hello. I may have excelled in the workforce as a reliable and efficient employee with a solid work ethic, but being a woman — an ethnic woman — became an impediment and limited my options. When I retreated to the Japanese community, I was at times considered brash and abrasive, a pariah: I boldly looked my elders in the eyes and did not bow my head or lower my gaze. I spoke directly and in my frank alto rather than the expected high-pitched, singsong, or chirpy childlike manner. Outspoken and willing to argue about something I believed in, I refused to be silenced or dismissed. I became indignant when dealing with that dying breed of older Japanese men who spoke to young women like me as if we were children or patted us on the head like we were dogs.

For people like my grandparents, the old ways mattered. There were rules to be followed, traditions observed, status quo maintained, and strict hierarchies of rank and position. My ancestors knew their place and what was expected of them. Every generation feels compelled by a sense of pride, duty, accountability, and responsibility to pass on their legacy in some way. As a young woman, I resisted their lessons and rejected the notion I should carry on as they did. After all, to be a Japanese woman in the patriarchy placed you on the bottom tier, and a biracial woman fell much lower than that.

For years I tried to discard these ideas, but now acknowledge they are actually a part of me. My Japanese heritage felt like a double-edged sword — a centuries-long, rich history full of honour cloaked in inequitable cultural traditions. As much as I love my family, instead of transforming into a graceful swan, I grew into an angry young woman when my achievements were diminished by those whom I held most dear. Regardless of effort or whatever my accomplishments, I was not the one who mattered because of my gender. Only the men counted. I had always prided myself on being the first grandchild to graduate from university until hearing Grandma proudly boast that cousin Bryan was the first.

"Don't you remember Grandma, I was the first ..." I began.

Annoyed, she brushed aside my interruption and continued, "Yes, he was the first *grandson*."

Her words cut me to the core. Like succession lines in Japan, the highest status in many JC families is granted to the first-born male. Never mind how many women came before or after. For the men in my family, their accomplishments were considered worthier and their pursuits of much greater importance. That was just the way things were — and to some degree, they still are. Not long ago, Dee confided to me: "Growing up, I never felt like I mattered to anyone." "You mattered to us," I said.

When my grandfather was alive, he always sat at the head of the table and no one ever considered sitting in his chair. Starting with him, the men were always served first. The male relatives, including the non-Japanese husbands, and friends flocked to the choice seats flanking Grandpa to enjoy this preferential treatment as honoured guests. However, behind this show of deference lay another power structure: the rigid rule of women. The true heart of any home is the kitchen. For us girls, conscription to the kitchen began at an early age. Pressed into service, like the generations of women who came before us, we must toil and serve to fulfill our lifetime of duty: roll the sushi, present the food, pour the tea, wash the dishes. Unlike my male cousins, I'm expected to run through the trenches from kitchen prep to head cook, to be assigned to event planning and hostess duties, entrusted to do the shopping, or relegated to the cleaning crew.

Somehow domestic servitude came to represent family loyalty. This idea was imposed on us and determined our worth regardless of other contributions. Compelled by love and respect, I continue to help out of my own volition. In my mind loyalty means putting others' needs ahead of one's own, acting out of love — not from an embittered position of malice, the false face of martyred duty, or a show of effort for the sake of appearances. The older women in my family and the JC community at large may have accepted their roles with pride and grace, but an outlier like me could never comply with this lack of freedom and autonomy. Even if we shared the pain and experience of being considered second-rate in our own homes, instead of supporting one another or banding together, we often worked against each other.

Pity any Asian woman who fails on the home front. For it is there, in the household, where women are judged. Not by the men but by other women. Our merits or hindrances tested and proved, not by academic standards, community alms, or spiritual devotion, but through mundane tasks. Our culinary repertoire and prowess scrutinized; artistry and creativity measured through sewing and craft projects; organizational skills weighed by housekeeping and event planning; discipline observed through obedient children reared.

Different treatment exists for a woman who is considered physically attractive. For any woman willing to play the pretty girl role, a slew of other options become available provided genetics align in her favour. Every culture has its own popular notions and standards of beauty. For my father, it meant having blond hair and blue eyes; on my mother's side, idealized Japanese beauty included long bone-straight jet-black hair, porcelain skin, almond eyes with an eyelid crease, and a soft-spoken and quiet demeanour.

Instead of delving into the domestic arts, a woman could spend hours of dedicated effort studying the art of makeup application and figure-enhancing fashions to garner attention, reap benefits, and open doors. Attractive people in general have often enjoyed preferential treatment, higher status, or advantages over others simply because of their physical appearance, but this route is an equally hazardous playing field. It's a slippery slope where gravity invariably sets in. Hopefully, there's something sustaining and of substance behind this mask of beauty.

Thanks to my father's ugly duckling story, I never put much stock in my looks and avoided defining my identity by these parameters. Instead, I focused on developing practical skills and knowledge. I often refer to myself as the hag of Strathearn, which is in reference to the street bordering the local park and an accurate description of my current role. Most mornings, as I trudge through the wooded areas with my dog, Ivy, my makeup-less face is concealed behind dark sunglasses and errant locks stuffed under a large floppy hat. In contrast to the designer tracksuits or fashionable casuals my neighbours don, I'm consistently found in muddied and rough-worn dog-walking clothes. Sometimes I think I should make a greater effort and work on my appearance, but as an older woman, who's really looking at me anyway?

• • •

My aunts and cousins were members of the Sansei Choir and Dancers. As representatives from the JC community, they had the opportunity to participate in festivals like Nationbuilders, which was one of the first large events highlighting Toronto's multicultural community and marked a shift to bring other cultures into the limelight. Auntie Marlene still has the original programs and pamphlets[5] outlining its origins and how Leon Kossar produced the Nationbuilders program with his wife, Zena, who acted as production assistant.

Kossar, a Ukrainian Canadian, cofounded the Canadian Folk Art Council in 1964. The former *Toronto Telegram* columnist often reported on immigrant stories and became well-versed in the challenges these communities faced. Organized by the Community Folk Arts Council, the Nationbuilders festival introduced Toronto audiences to different ethnic groups. The event ran from 1966 to 1969 as part of the fun summer activities held at the annual CNE Grandstand in Toronto.

Following the success of Nationbuilders, the Kossars cofounded Toronto's Festival Caravan in 1969, simply known as Caravan[6] to most people. Visitors could purchase a small booklet designed to look like a real passport. Filled with a list of locations, addresses, and maps, these passports provided unlimited admission to every pavilion throughout the festival. When visitors arrived at each pavilion, passports were stamped, and guests were greeted by an honorary mayor and princess. The event ran for about nine days each June and showcased different cultures from around the world. With more than thirty international pavilions located throughout the Greater Toronto Area, various language groups and cultural communities restyled themselves as entertainment hubs and arts attractions. In a way Caravan helped change the face of Toronto. The annual

The Japanese Canadian Cultural Centre on Wynford Drive decked out as the popular Tokyo pavilion.

event arrived at a time when, instead of being the object of curiosity or scorn, it felt cool to be different. Proud communities like ours were making strides in the 1970s and 1980s by introducing new faces and traditions to a white majority hungry to enjoy different foods and culture.

Each summer at Caravan, the JCCC's Tokyo pavilion became a mecca for many Torontonians. For some patrons, it may have been their first introduction to Japanese food and the arts through live dance and music performances. The JCCC's president fell easily into the requisite mayor's role, but they still needed to find someone to act in this new princess role — a Miss Tokyo. Community groups participating in Caravan were enlisted to put forth suitable candidates aged 19 to 25 to compete in an event called the Princess Ball. Initially held at the upscale Westin Prince Hotel (now known as the Pan Pacific Toronto) in Don Mills, this semiformal evening attracted hundreds of supporters and guests and included dinner and dancing. After introductions each participant gave a speech about their interests and involvement in the community and then answered an identical set of questions posed by the master of ceremonies. The selected MCs, who were usually community members, and judges from outside the community made the final selection. The judges were a mix of both Japanese and non-Asians: company execs, modelling agents, and print and TV personalities.

Though never overtly stated, the Princess Ball, with its use of pageantry to select and crown a princess, sought out attractive women: "Selected for her personality and appearance, Miss Tokyo acts as a goodwill ambassador for the JCCC while attending many events throughout the city during the year."[7] To lure some of the best-looking women to participate in the ball, elaborate prizes were sought and dangled: an all-expenses-paid trip, fur coats, diamond jewelry, stereo systems, gift certificates, crystal stemware, and more. The winner received the lion's share of the best prizes, valued between $3,000 and $10,000, including a trip to São Paulo, Brazil, where she represented Canada in the Miss Nikkei International beauty pageant. Lesser but equally extensive prize packages were awarded to the first and second runners-up. Following the ball Miss Tokyo and the pavilion's mayor made appearances at the pre-Caravan press party and post-Caravan awards banquet, where all the Caravan princesses competed for the title of Miss Caravan.

News quickly spread each year whenever a family member participated and took home some great prizes. Grandma danced with a group of older adults called the Hi Fu Mi Steppers. These ladies specialized in line dances as well as some Japanese folk dances and performed at various events. They picked Dee as their representative in 1988, a natural choice known for her glamorous appearance and fashionable ways. In the entry package materials, a letter was sent to contestants: "Remember that this is not a beauty contest. The prime purpose is to select Miss Tokyo for the duration of Caravan. Her duties as well as those of the hostess is to represent the J.C. Community. Criteria for selection is based upon such intangible traits as poise, charm and communication skills."

Fashion magazines and films started to include mixed race models and actors, yet Dee and I knew JCs like us, whatever the label — biracial, hapa, hāfu, or Eurasian — didn't stand a chance. One look at us and we'd instantly be judged as not Japanese enough. Only a fully Japanese woman would ever win. Despite this, Dee placed first runner-up. She remembers how several people made a point of approaching her after the decision to say, "We really thought you should have won." As it turned out, once Caravan rolled around, Dee ended up filling most of the hosting duties when the winner suddenly became unavailable.

Two years later, in 1990, Dee's old school friend Linda Kitagawa, now a radio host, shared the MC duties with actor Denis Akiyama in the JCCC auditorium, where the event migrated to. That same year Grandma put my name forward to the Hi Fu Mi Steppers group to run as their representative. Out of the seven contestants, two of whom I knew from my odori group, I somehow managed to place second runner-up. Neither

With Grandma at the Miss Tokyo 1990 pageant.

I nor Dee had wanted to participate, but we couldn't say no to Grandma. As family matriarch she had the prerogative to do whatever she deemed fitting. She acted first by submitting our names and told us about it later. Mom and other family members were instrumental on the original organizing committees, so it would have looked bad for us to refuse. We couldn't let the family lose face.

The Princess Ball required contestants to wear kimono. *Here's my chance to finally look the part*, I thought. Sometimes a girl just wants to look good. When I was a dancer, I always wanted to get that classic updo, what I imagined as the ultimate Japanese hairstyle and the epitome of Japanese beauty. But that style remained reserved for the favourite dancers, chosen to portray delicate geisha, and not for those of us who were cast as rough men. Someone suggested an *ijūsha* hairdresser they knew. Certainly, I reasoned, a new immigrant from Japan would be an expert in styling Japanese hair — she'd know exactly what to do.

At the time I didn't know the Japanese word for the hairstyle I wanted was *shimada*, an elaborate hairstyle popularized during the Edo period (1603–1868) that featured "wide parts to the sides by the ears and was pulled up into a bun at the top or back."[8] The hairdresser's name has conveniently slipped my mind. I tried my best to describe what I wanted, but she spoke limited English and had no idea what I was talking about. Maybe she couldn't understand why I wanted an old-fashioned hairstyle. She knew I needed to wear kimono. That much I explained successfully.

Instead, I left the salon with a matronly version of a bun and pin curls around my face, looking nothing at all like what I had hoped for. Quite hideous really, but it was too late to salvage

Prior to the pageant, all Miss Tokyo 1990 candidates had a photo shoot.

things. Once I changed out of kimono that evening, my Western clothes severely clashed and made me look even more ridiculous. Some beauty queen. Thinking back I now see odori as a finishing school of sorts for the scores of young JC women, including myself and other contestants. Those many years of dancing had instructed us on how to wear a kimono with grace and poise and encompassed the special attention to makeup and hair — all of it had prepared us to play this future role of an exotic hostess.

• • •

Click, click, click, click.

Amplified by concrete walls, the sound of heels on the terrazzo floor echoes across the third floor. Perched on pumps, a Japanese woman teeters along with delicate birdlike steps. Immediately, I recognize she's *shin ijūsha* — a postwar immigrant and recent arrival from Japan. In those days "Japanese Japanese" (a term we JCs used to call them) stood out, marked by their lack of Western mannerisms, different styles of clothing, and telltale makeup — white powdered face, lack of blush, and thickly crayoned reddish lipstick — offset by angular cropped black hair.

"Ah, hello," she says as she breezes in, her English heavily accented. Just as the French roll their *r*'s off the tongue, Japanese learning English commonly switch out their *l*'s for *r*'s. "Is this the office?"

Seated at the computer table in the JCCC's meeting room, I answer, "No, it's right across the hall."

"Wow! You have computer? Must be important work."

"I'm working on the Centre's newsletter. I'm the editor."

"Oh! You're English expert, specialist." She bobs up and down, reminding me of a chickadee in motion. Tilting her head quizzically, she studies me in an effort to place me. "What is your interest in Japanese culture?"

I pause for a moment and wonder, *How many times must I be asked this loaded question?* "I'm part Japanese ..." I reply. I can already tell from the puzzled look on her face that my answer is unfathomable to her.

"Really?" Eyes narrowed, she leans forward and slowly inches toward me, scrutinizing. Then just as hastily as she arrived, she snaps back upright, turns, and flies off toward the office. From the distance I can hear what sounds like relief in her voice as she speaks Japanese with the ladies in the office. Strange as these newcomers seemed to us, we were equally alien to them.

• • •

Edith Maud Eaton knew first-hand how it felt to be viewed through a skewed filter, a specimen under glass. Using the pen name Sui Sin Far, Edith became one of the first writers to address controversial anti-Asian sentiments and explored themes of prejudice, oppression, and intermarriage in her writings about culture and community. Born in Britain, she and her family emigrated to New York and then settled in Montreal around 1872. In "Leaves from the Mental Portfolio of an Eurasian," she wrote about the difficulty of being biracial and what that meant living in North America in 1890: "I do not confide in my father and mother. They would not understand. How could they? He is English, she is Chinese. I am different to both of them — a stranger, tho their own child."[9]

Edith's younger sister Winnifred enjoyed success using the pen name Onoto Watanna.[10] She assumed the persona of a Japanese writer to guard against the ongoing anti-Chinese sentiments and for a time moved in New York society as a glamorous exotic. In contrast, Edith — often passing as white — travelled extensively through her supplementary work as a stenographer and gained access to Chinese communities within the U.S., shedding light on the plight of Eurasians who were often isolated and without connection to either Asian or white communities. She noted, "Fundamentally, I muse, people are all the same. My mother's race is as prejudiced as my father's. Only when the whole world becomes as one family will human beings be able to see clearly and hear distinctly. I believe that some day a great part of the world will be Eurasian."[11]

According to the 2016 Statistics Canada census, almost half of all Canadians acknowledge different ethnic origins, with four in ten people reporting more than one origin. A National Association of Japanese Canadians (NAJC) report[12] revealed JCs have a much higher intermarriage rate than other Canadians. In 2011 about 80 percent of JC couples included non-JC partners, and our interethnic marriage rate continues to increase. No doubt many of these individuals and their offspring share or can at least relate to my dilemma and feelings of displacement, exclusion, or racism.

For the JC community, with its high rate of intermarriage, that future is rapidly overtaking us. How far we've come, yet many things remain the same. I, too, have imagined that brave new world that accepts and celebrates biracial people — not the society of misfits or space-age aliens characterized by sci-fi narratives but as a modern-day reality. Where is that flock of accepting, beautiful people, the happily ever after from my father's original fable? Perhaps we're all still hiding in the wings, clinging to the shadows, hesitant to show our faces.

Court is a study in glass and metal featuring enormous expanses of light-filled space and bleached wood. Years have passed since its familiar surroundings encompassed our daily routines and etched themselves into Camille's memory. We let our family membership lapse, and it has been some time since we visited or attended any events.

Crossing the parking lot, we see clumps of people milling about and navigate our way around lineups for food vendors. Randomly scattered trucks attract patrons who wait patiently for their turn at the window, eager to sample their wares. A crowd is gathered in front of a makeshift stage area. Behind it wooden slats from the fence provide a backdrop and there's also a pop-up tent filled with equipment for the PA system. Wearing a black kimono, the announcer peers through his glasses, thoughtfully watching the performance as he stands beside a tidy row of the dancers' zori. He holds a microphone in one hand and his notes in the other, ever mindful of what's up next. In front of him, a couple of dancers stand on the sidelines, waiting for their cue to get into position for the next number.

Performing a stick dance with the Ayame-Kai troupe, Alana is already on stage. We made it just in time to see her dance for what might be the last time. From the two lines of dancers, all identically dressed in a white-turquoise-and-blue silk kimono with slim black obi, half had the red sleeves of their slip kimono exposed. We picked out our cousin immediately and as I scanned the other dancers, I recognized their faces — faces from the past. Standing in the audience, an awareness registered. I had come full circle: from spectator to performer and back to spectator again. Watching the dancers, I couldn't remember what those navy-and-white-striped wooden sticks were called or what they were supposed to represent. I wondered if I ever knew. It seemed strange to me now why I never questioned these things when I was on the stage.

It's been years since we attended the summer festival, or Natsu Matsuri. Our annual family picnic in July always conflicts with the date. And rather than switch one weekend for the next, my family is resistant to changing our traditions even though it means some family members will have to miss out because they need to choose between attending one or the other. Luckily for us, since our immediate family were not the hosts in 2019, the picnic ended in the early afternoon. Instead of feeling obligated to stay behind until after dinner, we rushed back to the city to catch the performances.

Camille and I congratulate Alana as she runs past us with the other dancers. "Did you see me trip on the floorcloth?" Alana asks, laughing.

"No, we must have missed that part," I say.

Alana is my first cousin. She's the daughter of Aunt Norma, who is my mom's youngest sister. In our family each generation is heavily weighted as either male or female. My mother is the oldest of her six sisters and one brother. Of the thirteen grandchildren, there are only four females among nine males. And so far, among the nine great-grandchildren, seven are girls and two are boys. Born twenty-four years after me, Alana was the first girl after a run of eight boys. All of us showered the adorable bundle of energy with attention and encouraged her when she began to pursue dance. Alana's father is a mix of Scottish and Irish. Like me, she spent many of her early years at the JCCC. She's also the sign of the Horse and has always been cheerful and energetic. By grouping family members by their Chinese zodiac sign, we need to determine only how many twelve-year cycles we are apart in age.

Alana performs a samurai dance in the mid-2000s.

When I ask about her formative years, Alana thinks she was five or six years old when she began jazz, tap, ballet, acrobatics, and Scottish Highland dancing on top of odori. By the time she was about nine, she had begun to dance competitively in tap and jazz, winning a few medals. One day her schoolteacher pulled her aside and lectured Alana about falling behind in her classes because she was spending too much time focused on dancing and not enough on homework or school. Her teacher suggested she quit all extracurricular activities, unaware how important these were to Alana. Embarrassed, Alana rushed home and said to her mom, "I want to stop everything but odori."

One reason Alana wanted to continue odori was the connection to our Japanese heritage. Alana remembers seeing how happy Grandma was whenever she danced, and it was something she wanted to hold on to. Alana also grew up seeing photos of her mom as a young girl in kimono from her early dancing days. For her, knowing her mom wanted her to share that experience and be part of the next batch of dancers felt like she had completed another cycle in our family's history.

Alana enrolled with the Ayame-Kai dance troupe, led by Susan Nikaido. Susan was a fellow dance member when her mother, Barbara, was one of my teachers at Haru-Yagi Kai. The group's name was changed after my great-aunt Harumi retired. In contrast to the more active and emotive styles of Western dance, classical Japanese dance follows a different, more solemn aesthetic. Alana recalls her early lessons and having to temper her approach and enthusiasm: "My dance teacher would always tell me 'Remember, odori is [about] being still and graceful and you can't jump around like you jump around in jazz,' cause I guess I had more spunk when I did odori — I was more bouncy." There's also a tradition of maintaining a composed expression; her teacher often reminded her, "There's no smiling."

For twenty more years, Alana stuck with it. Dance highlights include participating in the Red-and-White musical competition (a.k.a. Kohaku Utagassen), the Road to Asia Festival, and a special audience with the emperor and empress of Japan when they visited the JCCC in 2009. Her dedication was rewarded in 2014 when Susan Nikaido nominated Alana for the Nisei Veterans' Award.[1] Launched by the JCCC in 2006, the purpose of the award is to remember the dedication and loyalty of nisei veterans to Canada during the Second World War. The award recognizes youth aged 15 to 25 who participate in martial arts or odori programs and exemplify nisei values of loyalty, integrity, perseverance, good citizenship, determination, courage, service, and participation. In writing an essay on what receiving the award meant to her, Alana highlighted the importance of growing up in the JC community:

> I'm so proud to be Japanese Canadian, but the reason why is because my grandma is proud to be Japanese Canadian, and she has in a way showed all of us, the family that we should never be ashamed of who we are. And we should stick with our heritage even if people look down on it. We should just be who we are. My grandma did odori, my mom did odori and I'm doing odori; it's just part of our heritage, part of who we are and because of my grandma's strong influence, it's what made me so proud to be Japanese Canadian.

In 2016 Alana also received a Volunteer Award for Arts and Culture in Toronto, which is "awarded annually by the Government of Ontario, Ministry of Citizenship and Immigration, in recognition of the commitment and dedication by volunteers with more than five years of continuous service."[2] The JCCC submits nominations under the categories of operations, special events, art and culture, and youth. Aunt Norma won that same year in the special events category for her ongoing service to the community.

For now Alana's dancing days have ended. The graphic artist, designer, and illustrator moved from Toronto to Ottawa near the end of 2019 to take advantage of the lower living costs while creating a board game about dreams. She didn't connect with the JC community or the dance scene in Ottawa. Although there are activities affiliated with both the Ottawa Japanese Community Association, established in 1976, and the Ottawa Japanese Cultural Centre. Alana returned to Toronto in April 2021 to be closer to family and continues to work on the board game, with plans to reconnect with her close friends from the Ayame-Kai.

· · ·

After the classical odori numbers finish, Camille and I wander inside the JCCC to look around at the booths. Stepping back outside into the parking lot, we run into Grandma and Aunt Yuki, who also headed to the Centre after the picnic to enjoy the Natsu Matsuri festivities. At ninety-eight, Grandma is still sharp as ever but isn't as able-bodied and needs a walker to get around. For outings she uses her wheelchair. Despite the warm summer evening, Grandma is wearing a pale-yellow cardigan,

It's been decades since the bon odori was held downtown at city hall, now known as Nathan Phillips Square. From more than 400 attendees in the early 1970s, numbers had dwindled to about 150 in 1981. Since Obon is traditionally celebrated in July, for many years bon odori festivities were scheduled on the second weekend of the month. After a scheduling conflict with the large-scale Toronto Outdoor Art Fair (formerly known as the Toronto Outdoor Art Exhibition), which attracted high-profile people in the arts scene, the city asked the dance groups to switch their date to accommodate the event.

Cousin Eleanor and other dancers remember how bon odori moved around for years before merging with Natsu Matsuri at the JCCC in 2002, where it continues to be celebrated. From downtown Toronto the Obon Odori performances migrated to North York. Mel Lastman Square opened in 1989, and on July 14, 1990, about seventy-five dancers performed there for the first time. Each of the four major bon odori groups were represented: Ayame-Kai, Sakura Kai, Suzuran-Kai of Hamilton, and the TBC. Although they remained there for several years, I never managed to see any performances before they changed locations again. One dancer recalled a brief stint at Albert Campbell Square at Scarborough City Hall, including one year when they danced indoors due to bad weather. A couple of years later, they were off to North York Civic Centre until the citywide garbage strike in 2002 cancelled all activities.

When the Obon organizers reached out to the community to find yet another location, the JCCC welcomed them to join its first summer festival, Natsu Matsuri.[3] From 2002 onward, they performed outside the Garamond Court building in Don Mills. Camille and I attended some of these earlier summer celebrations. They were quiet events then; I remember a practically empty parking lot and barely a handful of people in attendance. Back at the old Centre, whenever we attended Haru Matsuri or Caravan, you just had to look around and you'd recognize most of the people. At this venue, we noticed most patrons were modern-day *ijūsha*. New varieties of booths had emerged, catering to the increase in Japanese-speaking groups and indicating the growing popularity and shifting tastes toward contemporary Japanese culture. Gone were the familiar JC versions of tempura and chicken teriyaki dinners so popular in the past. Instead, they'd been replaced by more authentic Japanese cuisine: summer staples like a somen noodle bar and gigantic shaved ices known as kakigōri — a Japanese version of our snow cones but with flavours like green tea and melon.

• • •

Reflecting on that day at Natsu Matsuri, I'm engulfed in reminiscing. Memories of these and other community events held at former locations seep back into my consciousness only to be washed away by the reality of what was before me. Taking in and absorbing the spectacle, I remember feeling momentarily thrown off balance in encountering those colliding landscapes of past and present, familiar and strange. There's a sense of erasure and loss when former places, steeped in history, no longer remain as they once were. In my mind I can still see these old haunts; they exist in my memory but are now lost to time and space. The shifting sands of change are disruptive and unsettling.

By unearthing these snapshots of the past, my thoughts turn to questions of identity. To relive these events and examine them from a different vantage point requires excavating years of emotional debris, whether we're conscious of this clutter or not. To avoid clouded vision, it's essential to remove the tinted lens of sentimentality for clarity to emerge. In doing this we're faced with hard truths of reality. Collectively, we have been raised by a community of trauma survivors. Dr. Kerry Ressler,[4] a psychiatry professor at Harvard Medical School, says children who experience family separation or have a household member incarcerated face an increased risk of long-term mental and physical health problems. This childhood trauma is considered a risk factor for myriad issues from adult depression to obesity, cancer, heart attack, and stroke. Research shows it's common for people to try and escape traumatic memories by drinking, smoking, using drugs, and overeating. Physically, stress and anxiety affect the body, which can lead to cardiovascular and autoimmune diseases. While denial and avoidance are seen as coping mechanisms, past traumas can be treated, says Ressler. Those who have faced trauma are known to pass problems on to other family members, so by addressing your own problems, you could end up helping others.

Does the past define who we are, who we become? The war shattered the JC community and its splintered groups were forced to scatter across Canada. People like my grandparents, who settled in Toronto, were careful not to become a target again and resisted congregating in any one area of the city. Rather than look for answers or alternative narratives, or address any type of individual or collective healing, as survivors they were more focused on trying to rebuild their lives and care for their families, even if they felt stigmatized long after their release.

In her research of wartime narratives of JC women, sociologist Pamela Sugiman observed a "heightened sense of loss" in speaking with many JCs. "When I asked them to sum up their stories as a way of concluding their narratives, most women tempered personal pain and critical thought with the passage of time. They minimized the suffering of the past with the successes, comforts, and contentment of the present. The voices of the present offered forgiveness, perhaps for the preservation of dignity."[5]

Though everyone responds differently to trauma, these unfathomable experiences changed the course of people's lives and resulted in feelings of anxiety and shame that bind us all to the past. Whether JCs spoke of it or not, these effects influenced the upbringing of generations that followed and the question of trauma remains.

What does it mean to be Japanese? Older JCs often referred to themselves as Nikkei. This word holds multiple meanings and differs from the term *Nihonjin*, which refers to Japanese nationality. Following a three-year study, one hundred scholars from ten countries and fourteen institutions collaborated on the International Nikkei Research Project, which debated and probed these questions of identity. Based on their findings, they came up with the following definition: "Nikkei identity is not static. It is a symbolic, social, historical, and political construction. It involves a dynamic process of selection, reinterpretation, and synthesis of cultural elements set within the shifting and fluid contexts of contemporary realities and relationships. These relationships have had a long history intensified within the current context of global capitalism. As Nikkei communities form in Japan and throughout the world, the process of community formation reveals the ongoing fluidity of Nikkei populations, the evasive nature of Nikkei identity, and the transnational dimensions of their community formations and what it means to be Nikkei."[6]

Sitting down to breakfast on June 20, 2020, Camille noticed an online post for International Nikkei Day, also known as International Day of Nikkei.[7] The idea is said to have originated from two third-generation Okinawan descendants: Andrés Higa from Argentina and Tadashi Andrés Ysa Urbina from Peru, who were students when they attended a reunion in Okinawa, Japan. Wanting to regain their roots, they were successful in having October 30 declared as Worldwide Uchinanchu Day to recognize Uchinanchu, which refers to Okinawan natives. From there they pushed for another event to unite all people of Japanese origin. After they met an Argentinean Nikkei who represented Argentina in the Convención Panamericana Nikkei (COPANI), a.k.a. Pan-American Nikkei Convention, their proposal to have June 20 declared International Nikkei Day was accepted at the COPANI 2017 event held in Lima, Peru. COPANI is a Nikkei conference held every other year with delegates from all over the world. Outside of Japan, South America contains the largest population of Nikkei.

On June 6, 2018, the 59th Convention of Nikkei & Japanese Abroad, held in Honolulu, also declared June 20 as International Day of Nikkei. The association recognizes the historical date when the first Japanese immigrants landed in Hawaii in 1868. The declaration's final resolution reads: "The Gannenmono, the first immigrants from Japan, arrived in Hawaii on June 20, 150 years ago, which is a commemorable day when the Japanese went overseas for the first time in the modern history of Japan. Having shared the same Nikkei identity, we declare June 20 as the 'International Day of Nikkei' in order to express our appreciation for the efforts of the first generation, promote links and collaborations among Nikkei based on the Nikkei legacy of the world, thus contributing further to the international society."[8]

The Japanese Overseas Association[9] describes how the annual Nikkei conference is rooted in other acts of generosity. Thanks to efforts by the Red Cross, deliveries from Japan were made to Japanese Americans and nationals interned in various U.S.-based camps during the Second World War. In receiving familiar items such as miso, shoyu, and Japanese reading materials, former internees were determined to repay these acts of kindness after the war when Japan faced extreme shortages. Through various organizations, Christian church groups, and labour unions, a group called Licensed Agencies for Relief in Asia (LARA) was created in 1946 and provided humanitarian aid to a devastated Japan. LARA goods shipments, as they were known, sent gifts of food and clothing to Japan from 1946 to 1956. This example prompted other countries, including Canada, to start similar relief efforts through the Red Cross.

After being inducted into the United Nations on December 18, 1956, Japan decided to host an event in Tokyo to commemorate the occasion. The following May, the country formally expressed its gratitude to Nikkei immigrants for their support in Japan's recovery. By 1960 the festival was recast as a convention, and two years later, it became an annual event. The organizing board incorporated in 1967, and it continues to provide support to Nikkei immigrants.

What does it mean to be Nikkei? Peruvian sansei Roberto Oshiro Teruya summarizes it in the following terms:

> It encompasses a sentiment, shared values, many things in common such as customs and food, regardless of nationality. And we don't necessarily have the same physical characteristics, because many of us are multiracial. It

CHAPTER 11

ORDE STREET REVISITED

FROM BEHIND A wall of newsprint, a thin stream of smoke snakes its way up to the kitchen ceiling. A slender hand emerges and sets down a mug of black coffee. The sound of light tapping punctuates the rustling of newspaper as a tapered index finger reaches forward, releasing a lengthy cigarette ash into a growing cinder heap. Long manicured fingernails, painted a deep claret tone, elongate the elegant hand and provide contrast to the filthy overflowing ashtray. From within that sooty grey mound, a random cigarette butt ringed with dark red lipstick peeks out.

On one side of the narrow galley-style kitchen, days' worth of unwashed dishes line the kitchen countertop, jockeying for space in and around the single stainless-steel sink. Across from the block of cabinets and pushed up against the wall, a small oval Arborite table with metal legs is littered with stacks of mail, newspapers, and flyers. Sitting in her worn polyester robe, my mother is worlds away.

"Mom … Mom? … Mom!"

My questions are greeted with silence. Fuelled by an insatiable curiosity, there was always something to know and I wanted answers. I persist, asking again and again, louder and louder until I'm practically shouting. My mother routinely ignored me. Was it her way of avoiding questions or an attempt to silence me? I discovered I needed to be loud or shocking to garner attention. I grew into a loud talker to overcompensate for our crowded and boisterous family gatherings. Sure, some of my relatives were partially deaf and others had limited English skills, but I'm not sure why we thought increasing the volume would help with their comprehension.

As an adult it dawned on me one morning like a flashback to my youth. How many parents with young children have those moments when they suddenly gain some keen insight or understanding of their own parents? When I was the mother of a young child, I wanted nothing more than to indulge in the quiet pleasure of reading the weekend newspaper with a cup of coffee. Sitting at my own kitchen table, it occurred to me that perhaps my mother, as a single parent, was merely exhausted. Perhaps she had no answers or energy to respond to a barrage of childhood curiosity. Perhaps she needed to find her own private sanctuary somewhere far away from everyday life. Years of living with my quiet husband also proved instructive: his lack of a response when I spoke had the power to enrage me. In another aha moment, I realized this reaction hearkened back to those early childhood experiences.

• • •

Learning Japanese is hard. You would think I'd have an advantage from hearing Japanese spoken as a child when we lived with my grandparents. For the most part, everyday conversations took place in English, however broken, even for my mother's generation.

Our elders, the issei or nisei, habitually spoke Japanese to one another. They shared their first language with the rest of us by sprinkling in words here and there, usually for Japanese items or foods. We simply accepted these things. One example springs to mind: everyone called my great-grandmother Bāchan. As a child I thought it was her name. When I said this aloud everyone laughed heartily at my ignorance. How hilarious! Didn't I know, someone finally explained, "bāchan" means "grandmother" in Japanese? Despite my thirst for knowledge, a mental block kept foreign words and their meanings far from my grasp. My French Canadian husband has an amazing ear for languages. He only needs to hear a word to remember it. I've never been like that. My facility for other languages remains limited. I need to see things written down to really absorb them.

When we were kids, my mom enrolled us in the Toronto Japanese Language School (TJLS). I remember spending my time staring out the windows overlooking the playground. The Japanese language school rented space in Orde Street Public School. My teachers, all immigrants, spoke limited English. They tried their best to teach us by rote. Some theories claim if you hear another language long enough, you will eventually clue into its meaning. But apparently, this complete immersion approach takes time — the equivalent to a year in hours to become adequately proficient. (Although, after decades of living

in Canada, Bāchan never learned to speak English.) As one of
the few mixed kids who stood out in this sea of Japanese, I felt
alone and frustrated by my lack of understanding. I might have
been able to recite some things, but without detailed explanations, my comprehension was basically nil. As a top student at
my English public school, I had little patience for the slower
learners; yet here the roles reversed, and I found myself humili-
ated to be the class dunce.

I've heard new Canadians complain how hard it is to learn
English because of its bizarre spellings, use of homonyms, and
multiple meanings for the same word. Japanese is no different.
First you need to learn hiragana and then katakana — not
one but two phonetic alphabets. Also known collectively as
kana, each alphabet is comprised of forty-six characters; they
sound identical but are written differently. Katakana is used for
non-Japanese words imported from other languages. Children
in Japan learn both alphabets in elementary school. Added to
these kana are kanji — an estimated forty-six thousand characters imported from the Chinese language. Evolved from picto-
grams and conceived around 1400 BCE, kanji are complicated
to learn and write. Kanji can represent a single word, an entire
phrase, or multiple concepts and meanings. In newspapers and
other printed materials, kanji are combined with hiragana and
katakana. To become literate at an adult level of comprehension, you need to know between twenty-five hundred and three
thousand kanji. Grade school children learn about one thousand kanji and expand to two thousand before the end of high
school.[1] According to former teachers, the number of kanji that
exists is unknowable. There are ancient ways of writing Chinese
characters, which have fallen out of favour and are mainly of
interest to historians and scholars.

Growing up we learned the *wrong* Japanese from family and community members, not the *right* Japanese. Our words were incorrect, crude, backwards. We didn't know any better. As JCs we've lost our heritage language. Over the years I've met countless white people happy to instruct and correct: Japanese were this and that; this is how they lived; these were the foods they ate. These non-Japanese people spoke the language, studied the culture, and travelled extensively in Japan or lived there. Our experience didn't matter because they knew so much more. After all, we didn't speak Japanese and we hadn't been to Japan. Who were we to argue? They had us believe they were more Japanese than us. We JCs used the Japanese word for egg to describe these people as *tamagosan*. White on the outside, yellow on the inside. We didn't mean it in a derogatory way. Japanese culture has long attracted obsessive interest by individuals who used this term as a badge of honour. Countless Asian women have received much unwanted attention from these enthusiasts who seek them out. Some viewed these *tamagosan* as fetishists, and maybe they are.

Some JCs, like my grandfather, had the privilege of attending school in Japan, but not all his siblings had this opportunity. In larger centres like Vancouver, the community established local Japanese schools for those who could afford it. If you lived in the country, like my grandmother's family, most of the kids were too busy helping their parents on the farm to attend. Surrounded by a white majority in British Columbia, my grandparents' generation felt pressured to assimilate and understood the necessity of learning English.

The Second World War created a greater obstacle: entire generations had their education interrupted. Despite paying for public education through property taxes, JCs suddenly found their children yanked out of school. Countless youths saw their hopes for the future dashed as they were shuffled off to incarceration camps. Once these students were conveniently out of sight, the British Columbia government decided to shirk its responsibility to provide classes. The community rallied and former teachers like Hide Hyodo hastily assembled makeshift schools for primary students. The BC Security Commission conceded months later and provided a minimal level of support but remained steadfast in refusing secondary education to older students. Outside of the camps, few Canadians spoke out against the treatment of JCs. In *Ministry to the Hopelessly Hopeless*,[2] Roland Kawano details how groups like the Anglican, United, and Catholic Churches and the Woman's Missionary Society stepped in to voluntarily assist students taking correspondence courses, which allowed them to finish high school.

It's not surprising most people couldn't maintain their Japanese language studies during the war. Scores of individuals struggled to endure day-to-day living in small shacks without central heating, electricity, running water, or modern conveniences. Grandma had her first-born toddler, my mom, to look after and another baby on the way. Her days were filled with the time-consuming tasks of raising a family, handwashing laundry, hauling water, and preparing meals using a wood stove. Grandpa, and the few men who weren't in forced work crews or under guard as POWs, did labour-intensive jobs like chopping firewood for the entire camp. With so many other pressing priorities, few had the time, resources, or luxury to study Japanese.

• • •

I often wish I possessed more Japanese language skills. It certainly would have provided greater advantages and insights over the years. When Mia, my old friend from odori, heard I'd been laid off from the CBC, she encouraged me to apply for a position at Japanese Social Services (JSS), where she sat on the board.

Following a temporary closure, JSS began searching for an administrator, a new role marking a shift in operations. Formerly known as Japanese Family Services of Metropolitan Toronto and founded in 1987 by Hiroshima survivor Setsuko Thurlow, the organization provided much-needed counselling services to Japanese-speaking people. Within a few years, in 1990, it incorporated and became a nonprofit agency. Financial issues forced its doors to close for two years in 1996 and ended Thurlow's involvement. Board members pushed to reopen on a part-time basis before resuming full-time operations in 2000. They renamed the agency Japanese Social Services to reflect their expanded offerings.

Invited for a job interview, I strove to make a good impression. Wearing a pale-blue skirt suit, I offered a polite greeting in Japanese while formally bowing to the gathered board members. I was confident I had the necessary skills — in fact, I felt overqualified. During my early days at Citytv, one producer had called me Brainiac, a cartoon character I'd never heard of. Later, at the CBC, I was the go-to employee who never balked at taking on an extra shift or assignment. My willingness to navigate each challenge and resulting success helped propel me to the management ranks, a route that normally took decades to achieve, within a short time. But that dedication failed to shield me. In the year since my layoff, I had been unable to secure another job in the television industry, and I felt discarded, betrayed, and demoralized. Part of it was due to a shift in my mindset. After years of climbing the corporate ladder, I was no longer willing to sacrifice my personal life and well-being for my career. No one was more surprised by this transformation than me, but I happily traded the lure of an executive position for the promise of more family time. And in August 2000, I found myself knee-deep again in the JC community.

In February 2002 JSS received the Order of the Rising Sun, Silver Rays — a special honour awarded in the emperor of Japan's name to people or organizations providing some merit-worthy service. The Japanese consul general hosted the award celebration at his Forest Hill residence, where I finally met Setsuko Thurlow. Immediately, I recognized her from when she visited my high school decades earlier to share her story of being a schoolgirl when the atomic bomb dropped on Hiroshima. The horror of that day remained seared in her mind. Reliving the nightmare, she recounted being buried alive under rubble, struggling to free herself from darkness and move toward the light. Once outside she was greeted by charred bodies and the loss of family and friends. Despite this trauma she continued to speak out on the effects of radiation and campaigned tirelessly with the International Campaign to Abolish Nuclear Weapons — efforts recognized in 2017 when she jointly accepted the Nobel Peace Prize.[3]

Working at JSS provided a window into modern-day life in Japan via staff, board members, and many volunteers. Young women, most of whom were short-stay, work permit, and visa students, gravitated to the agency eager to access our information services and programs.

Seeing their advanced electronics and hearing about local festivals, fast-food offerings, wacky fads, and TV shows never ceased to amaze and entertain me. Reports emerged of ruthless Canadian employers and greedy landlords preying on and exploiting naive, trusting youth from Japan. Family and friends within the community were surprised to learn of any Japanese undergoing financial hardships. Japanese people were all well-off, weren't they?

At one board meeting, I suggested we start a holiday drive to help those who had fallen on hard times due to sickness, job loss, separation, or other family issues. The program, I explained, could mirror the Christmas hamper tradition, but instead of North American food staples, we'd fill them with Japanese groceries like shoyu and rice. The president thought the idea provided a wonderful grassroots approach, and the board wholeheartedly approved and supported this year-end gesture. Although Christmas is not a big holiday in predominantly Buddhist Japan, Toronto has more than half a dozen Japanese Christian congregations. I wasted no time in contacting local ministers, thinking these organizations might be able to assist us. Not only did every single church respond with offers to help, but they were also willing to work together for the common good despite their differences. And following the annual Joy of Christmas concert organized by this alliance of Christian churches, they donated the proceeds. Thanks to this ongoing support, the program continues to brighten the end of the year for its many recipients.

Conveniently located on the second floor of the new JCCC, JSS sat next door to the *Nikkei Voice* newspaper office, where I later divided my time as part-time managing editor. Renovations had transformed the first floor of the Garamond Court building into an oasis of Japanese-inspired design. In stark contrast the second floor awaited stage two of the Centre's development plans, and the tired grey surroundings resembled an abandoned warehouse space.

The sheer size of the building created many opportunities for a variety of disparate organizations, not originally associated with the JCCC, to meet under one roof. Ikebata Nursery School, one of the first tenants on the main floor, offered Japanese-style education for toddlers by teachers trained in the Japanese school system. The licensed daycare provided a Japanese-immersion setting, a niche not previously available to JCs. As parents we always want the best for our children and strive to give them every opportunity — particularly ones we never had or wished we did. Although my husband and I were reluctant at first and uneasy about putting our almost three-year-old toddler into the care of others at such a young age, the familiar surroundings of the community hub put the whole family at ease and allowed for an easier transition to our new daily routine. I think Camille may have found comfort knowing Mom worked upstairs. And depending on the day, following afternoon pickup from Ikebata, they delighted JSS or *Nikkei Voice* staff by helping Mom in the office.

· · ·

Clang-clang, clang-clang, clang-clang.

The unmistakable sound of the brass bell: a marked pace, rhythm, and timing. Hearing this alert immediately pricked up our ears, and books in tow, we dashed to get to class on time. Terrazzo floors and concrete walls amplified the ringing as I bound up the stairs, pausing to catch my breath on reaching the third floor. Mr. Tanaka seldom missed a day, dutifully walking the hallways, black handle in hand; swinging that

old-style school bell; and signalling to everyone that classes at
TJLS were about to begin. A thought enters my mind: *I'm too
old for this.* Yet here I found myself back at school.

When Camille was still in grade school, we spent several
years heading downtown to Orde Street Public School every
Saturday morning when other people were sleeping in. The
TJLS program started in September and finished in June.
Classes ran from nine thirty to just before noon, with a mid-
morning recess. To raise extra funds, the school sold snacks and
refreshments outside the staff room, where I'd pop in to say hi
to Auntie Terry. My great-aunt could often be found working
away in the makeshift office. An active PTA member while her
four sons studied there, she remained a volunteer and established the Terry Nakamura Assistance Award, a monetary prize
to encourage Nikkei students to continue their cultural studies.
Outside of school and at family gatherings, Auntie Terry encouraged us in our Japanese studies, realizing how important
language skills were.

During assemblies in the auditorium, Mr. Tanaka set
up microphones and the technical systems. Although he
remained an ever-present fixture and support behind the
scenes, his wife, Toshie, provided the true face of the school.
Education trailblazer and long-time principal, Toshie Tanaka
presided at the helm from 1979 to 2012. During her remarkable thirty-three-year tenure, she transformed the small
community school into one of the most respected Japanese
language schools in Canada. Frail and slight in appearance,
Toshie inspired respect and admiration through her towering
example of dignified leadership. I remember seeing her in the
staff room during registration, where she personally enrolled
students and provided academic advice.

Born in 1923 as Dorothy Toshiye Okuno, Toshie became interested in teaching at a young age. Living in Vancouver's bustling JC community had its advantages with the historic Japanese Language School on Alexander Street, where she headed for a second round of classes after she finished her day at public school. The keen student, with encouragement from her high school principal, decided to pursue further studies in Japan. After graduating in 1940, she moved to Osaka for a three-year teacher's college program. Teaching credentials in hand, she easily found work at a local elementary school, but by then constant air raids forced students and staff to evacuate to Shikoku until the end of the Second World War. The war effectively severed all communication between Toshie and her family in Canada. She had no idea what became of her parents until after they were released from the incarceration camps and forced to relocate to London, Ontario. This news arrived in a long-awaited letter from her mother urging her to come home.

Work kept Toshie in Japan for the next seventeen years. When she returned to Canada in 1957, she arrived with her husband, Kamezo Tanaka, and their daughter. It wasn't until their second child, born in Canada, turned six that Toshie became involved with TJLS and returned to teaching. She enrolled her youngest daughter at the school in 1966 and, within a short time, began teaching grades one and two. Her goal had always been to teach language skills to young children. Toshie believed the school had an important duty to help educate people and create stronger ties between Canada and Japan. She understood the evolution of the JC community, witnessing first-hand the shift in school enrolment from mainly children to adults. In the school's fortieth-anniversary commemorative booklet, *Ayumi*, she wrote, "Today as Japanese Canadians are living in a Canadian environment, their first language is English. The use of Japanese in the nisei/sansei home has all but disappeared. Under these conditions, it's understandable that they have a difficult time trying to speak, read or understand Japanese, which is truly one of the most difficult languages to master."[4]

During the postwar era, the JC community struggled to settle in an unfamiliar environment without support. People were dejected and carried the shame of their incarceration. Discrimination remained rampant and those looking for lodging and work faced barriers and countless challenges. People from the school described those inhospitable days in *Ayumi*: "There was a stigma attached to anything and everything about Japan and being Japanese. Defeated and devastated, Japan was condemned as a barbaric country with little to offer a civilized community of nations. Many Japanese Canadians were influenced, even intimidated, by this climate of opinion. For some, being identified as Japanese was more than an embarrassment; it was an obstacle to acceptance and assimilation as Canadians."[5] Determined community members envisioned a different future for their children and persisted in overcoming several hurdles from obtaining funding, classroom space, and instructors to locating books and teaching supplies in a period before diplomatic relations between Canada and Japan were reestablished.

On September 11, 1949, the first Japanese language school to open after the war welcomed students eager to improve their written and spoken Japanese language skills:

> The Toronto Japanese Language School is one of the many surviving monuments to the courage, accomplishments and pride of the Japanese Canadian Community. The

Archie Nishihama, a teacher at the Toronto Japanese
Language School, composed the school song.

Japanese language teachers and began his foray into teaching
by September 1958. In a makeshift classroom above the Furuya
Trading Company store on Dundas Street West in Chinatown,
he pioneered the first adult classes from 1962 to 1967. From
this role Nishihama pivoted to a long teaching career with
TJLS and served as principal at the Orde Street Public School
from 1965 to 1976. Nishihama maintained his passion for
music by leading community groups like the Sansei Choir and

continuing to play and compose music. He entered the TJLS's song contest held in conjunction with its twentieth anniversary, and in March 1969 his music and lyrics were selected to become their *kohka*. This school song continues to be sung today.

• • •

Before K-pop enjoyed huge popularity outside of Asia, Kyu Sakamoto was the first Asian recording artist to reach number one in North America.[9] In 1961 he released the Japanese hit song "Ue O Muite Arukou" ("I Look Up as I Walk"), composed by Hachidai Nakamura with lyrics by Rokusuke Ei. It's a timeless classic about longing for a fresh start. After tremendous success in Japan, the song became known in North America as "Sukiyaki" and spent three weeks at the top of the American Billboard charts in June 1963. The song has nothing to do with sukiyaki, which is a Japanese variation of the one-pot meal. During a business trip, the chair of Pye Records, Louis Benjamin, happened to hear the song. Taken by the catchy tune, he pushed his own artists to create a new recording for his U.K.-based label. He renamed this English version by Kenny Ball and his Jazzmen after his favourite Japanese dish and it quickly sped to the top ten on the U.K. charts.

"Sukiyaki" must have struck a chord with a local DJ at a radio station in Pasco, Washington, who managed to dig up and air Sakamoto's original recording. It immediately garnered attention and listeners were hungry for more airplay. Capitol Records then bought the U.S. distribution rights and decided to scrap the Japanese title in favour of the name "Sukiyaki" since it was easier for English-speaking audiences to remember and pronounce. Though I prefer the jazzy version by Japanese singer Misora Hibari, "Ue O Muite Arukou" remains one of my favourite songs. Remakes continue to be made worldwide. An instrumental version reportedly became one of the first songs broadcast in outer space when it was played to NASA astronauts during a 1965 spaceflight on board *Gemini 7*.[10]

There's a bitter aftertaste when names are altered to make them more palatable to North American audiences. Similarly, derogatory food metaphors like "banana" or "Twinkie" — slurs for Asians considered assimilated or out of touch with their ethnic heritage — are just as debasing. Even Spanish and Portuguese Christian missionaries, the first westerners to arrive in Japan during the sixteenth century, were said to be so dumbfounded by the Japanese language they denounced it as "the devil's tongue."[11] Yet sometimes in our eagerness for acceptance, we may be reluctant to protest and quietly acquiesce even when feeling belittled or shortchanged — the result of absorbing decades of anti-Asian racism, which has seeped into our collective consciousness and sowed seeds of uncertainty. When you question your own abilities, it poisons your outlook and leads you to falsely believe others are more deserving or knowledgeable. I know there were times when, instead of asserting myself, I remained tied in place, kept back by the gatekeepers of the day. Instead of speaking out, I was quick to respectfully bow and retreat or politely step aside and forfeit my rightful place.

· · ·

In any language it's helpful to have the proper vocabulary. When we were younger, we lacked an adequate understanding of our history and didn't possess the current terms of reference. Words like "xenophobia" and "microaggression" weren't common or a part of the vernacular. If we were overlooked for a job or promotion, we rationalized that we were responsible: it was because we weren't good enough and had to work harder or needed to improve something about ourselves that was lacking.

The term "racial imposter syndrome" (RIS), coined by psychologists Suzanne Imes and Pauline Rose Clance, is similar to imposter syndrome, or imposter phenomenon. It is used as an explanation when a person doubts their abilities or to describe high achievers who are unable to accept their success and fear being exposed as a fraud. When combined with the element of race, the syndrome becomes more complex.

Kelly Bates, president of the Interaction Institute for Social Change, suggests assimilation and identity factor largely in imposter syndrome since racial minority groups must exert a disproportionate amount of effort into adapting and assimilating into mainstream culture to "become another version of yourself — watered down, less happy, more anxious, and constantly questioning your abilities."[12] Unlike their white counterparts, minorities may feel they face additional challenges to achieve success in North America: "This vice grip of assimilation and internalized inferiority finds us showing up as half of ourselves in the workplace."[13] Bates adds, "We may have the best idea in a meeting ... but we feel self-conscious advocating for it or even raising it. People may want us to take on leadership roles but we turn them down, either because we think we don't deserve the role or we might fail."[14] Our efforts to blend in and gain acceptance often mean erasing or discarding our own culture and identities. And ultimately, as a result, "racial imposter syndrome drains your confidence meter, and confidence is necessary to take risks, lead and collaborate with others."[15] Two factors causing RIS include being a minority and experiencing family pressure to achieve,

and some minority groups may be especially susceptible: "A 2013
study by researchers at the University of Texas at Austin surveyed
ethnic-minority college students and found that Asian-Americans
were more likely than African-Americans or Latino-Americans
to experience impostor feelings."[16] Mixed race individuals experience an additional layer of difficulty with RIS.[17] These individuals
often feel at odds with their own racial identity — they may feel
racially ambiguous or lacking in cultural knowledge or awareness,
particularly if their upbringing has focused on only one culture or
ethnic community. They may also feel unworthy or lack acceptance within one group. In some cases they might feel pushed to
choose or side with one ethnicity at the expense of another.

Beneath RIS and feelings of self-doubt lie deeper issues
informed by decades of oppression. It's easy to feel insecure
when you don't have the full picture or are missing key details.
Consider how oppressive societal forces, before and after the
Second World War, made it possible to strip JCs of their heritage language. The Toronto school curriculum failed to include
these pertinent facts; this Canadian history remains largely un-
told and continues to be erased from public consciousness. In
that destructive era, the Canadian government committed an
act of cultural genocide against JCs.

In 1993 American clinical psychologist Maria Root created
the following Bill of Rights for People of Mixed Heritage:

> I HAVE THE RIGHT ...
> Not to justify my existence in this world.
> Not to keep the races separate within me.
> Not to justify my ethnic legitimacy.
> Not to be responsible for people's discomfort
>   with my physical or ethnic ambiguity.

I HAVE THE RIGHT ...

To identify myself differently than strangers
    expect me to identify.

To identify myself differently than how my
    parents identify me.

To identify myself differently than my
    brothers and sisters.

To identify myself differently in different
    situations.

I HAVE THE RIGHT ...

To create a vocabulary to communicate about
    being multiracial or multiethnic.

To change my identity over my lifetime —
    and more than once.

To have loyalties and identification with more
    than one group of people.

To freely choose whom I befriend and love.[18]

This bill resonated with me from the first time I read it and articulates many issues I've grappled with. It's a helpful reminder: I don't need permission to be who I am.

• • •

If learning Japanese is hard, learning to communicate is harder.

Some people are always talking, but they rarely say anything meaningful. Fearful of encountering a moment of silence, they nervously strive to fill that space. It's comforting to be able to enjoy the company of others, sharing time without the need to speak. There is beauty in the unspoken word. My

Kokoro Dance Theatre Society during the late 1980s were greeted with standing ovations. The Vancouver-based troupe, founded in 1986 by Hirabayashi and his wife, Barbara Bourget, uses Eastern and Western aesthetics to create evocative performances. Included in the name is the Japanese word *kokoro*, which means "heart, soul, and spirit" because the duo wanted to "to express their humanity and emotions through motion."[1]

I remember the packed theatre full of JCs like me, eager to see ourselves reflected in new artistic works that explored our issues and mirrored the reality of our lives. Emboldened by the growing momentum of the JC redress campaign that began in 1984, we were no longer content to be marginalized by stereotypical tokenism or the lack of representation in mainstream media — we wanted our own stories told. For many of us, Hirabayashi's performance was our first exposure to butoh, or what is sometimes dubbed "the dance of darkness,"[2] an extreme art form and avant-garde combination of modern dance and theatre. Butoh originated in Japan during the late 1950s through the pioneering works of founders and collaborators Tatsumi Hijikata and Kazuo Ohno, and it evolved further during the 1960s and 1970s. Butoh is unmistakable with its slow, precise movements, primal contorted faces, and scantily clad bodies liberally covered in white makeup.[3] Certainly not the Japanese dance I knew but emotionally charged, shocking, and exhilarating.

After attending a performance in 1980, Jay Hirabayashi and Barbara Bourget were inspired to research the form. This pivotal moment became the foundation of their future work. Around the same time, organizations like the Canada Council for the Arts were making strides to highlight Canada's diversity and providing grants for artists outside the mainstream, including Hirabayashi, who received funding to launch his dance company. Through the efforts of Kokoro Dance, the butoh tradition in Canada continues.[4]

In an interview with the *Bulletin* editor John Endo Greenaway, Hirabayashi offers these insights: "For metaphoric reasons, butoh dancers often paint themselves white. It's a way of erasing yourself in order to express something that transcends yourself…. A butoh dancer changes time and space by changing your interior sense of time and space. Often, butoh appears slow to the observer, but inside the butoh dance is traveling very fast. So fast that the body has to struggle with the resistance of its own speed."[5] He adds, "Butoh is the search for one's own original expression. As SU-EN, a Swedish butoh dancer, once said, it is an impossible search. Life is a process where the more you learn, the less you realize you know."[6]

As a Japanese American, Hirabayashi wanted to inform audiences about the internment, taking inspiration from his father's incarceration for disobeying curfew and evacuation orders during the Second World War. In 1942 Gordon Hirabayashi, a twenty-three-year-old student at the University of Washington, had the courage to defy internment orders. Decades later, in the 1980s, historical evidence surfaced to reveal how the U.S. government withheld or knowingly falsified key evidence during the original trial. This led to *Hirabayashi v. United States*, a landmark court case where his wartime convictions were finally overturned. At the time of the ruling, Hirabayashi said, "The Constitution does not mean anything unless it can stand up in a time of crises. In 1942 the whole system of government failed us."[7] After his death in 2012, Gordon Hirabayashi was posthumously awarded the Presidential Medal of Freedom by President Barack Obama.

Butoh has a way of remaining with the viewer. Eury Chang saw the Vancouver premiere of *Rage* in 1986. Thirty years later the performance stayed with him: "The most memorable moment of the evening remains burned on my mind's eye: near the end, Jay Hirabayashi was blindfolded, and his mouth remained agape in a silent scream. His physical and facial gestures captured the pain and patience of Japanese internees, offering his audiences a reminder and mirror of this dark moment in Canadian history."[8]

Chang's extensive writings include Kokoro Dance's history and its groundbreaking debut in Canadian dance. The adjunct professor at the University of British Columbia spent many years researching and documenting Asian Canadian dance and theatre. In *Contemporary Directions in Asian American Dance*, Chang examines how the shifting political climate influenced Canada's funding of the arts, which in part led to the development of Kokoro Dance's inaugural performance, "a dance work that clearly uses choreographed movement, costume, and music to explore issues of social injustice, the politics of identity, and place."[9] Positioned far from commercial dance culture or idealized images of pretty Asian dancers, butoh's intense aesthetic focuses on internal imagery and emotional integrity. As Chang observes, "This outsider status and distance also provide the company's choreographer with enough distance from which to critique the values of mainstream culture, which have sought to *racialize* and *otherize* Japanese Canadians."[10]

· · ·

During the early 1980s, JC community activists began meeting in small groups across Canada. Sharing their stories of wartime internment and relocation, and the resulting trauma and shame these experiences had on them, fuelled a common desire for redress. A movement began, led by the National Association for Japanese Canadians (NAJC) and with the Toronto chapter playing a key role. The JC redress campaign spurred community members into action. It became a galvanizing force in its fight to hold the government of Canada accountable for the human rights violations enacted upon JCs during the Second World War.

In Toronto, activist and author Joy Kogawa stressed the need for a better means of communication to continue the campaign's momentum. In December 1987 she helped found *Nikkei Voice*, a bimonthly national newsletter, and remained one of the editorial advisors. In the fifteenth-anniversary tribute edition, *Nikkei Voice*'s first Japanese editor, Tomoko Makabe, describes those beginnings and how Kogawa "frantically phoned her friends and associates all over the country to raise money to start a new organization."[11] From its inception in the Toronto NAJC's office, the original *Nikkei Voice* mailing list included around thirteen thousand households across Canada. Just about every JC household received the free publication, including ours. Crammed with all things JC, the paper included updates on the redress campaign. Throughout the years, the masthead continues to read like a who's who in the JC community and many prominent individuals pledged their support from the very beginning. As Makabe reminisced, "Once, I recall, we had the late Ken Adachi at one of our editorial meetings and he indicated his support for redress and the idea of a new community forum."[12]

Like other ethnic groups, communities like ours wanted to see ourselves reflected in the city's governance, so it was an important acknowledgment of our changing society when Canada passed the Canadian Multiculturalism Act on July 21, 1988. The act helped pave the way forward for redress in that it recognizes the importance of preserving, sharing, and enhancing the cultural heritage and racial and ethnic diversity of all the country's citizens. At long last the decades of persistent calls for justice within the JC community were gaining traction and led to Prime Minister Brian Mulroney's historic apology to JCs on September 22, 1988. In addition to the apology and $21,000 compensation for each internment survivor, $24 million went to create the Canadian Race Relations Foundation and $12 million went into a community fund managed by the NAJC.[13] JCs stood clapping and cheering in the gallery at the announcement, while on the floor NDP leader Ed Broadbent paused, overcome with emotion, and read from Joy Kogawa's *Obasan*: "I cannot bear the memory.... There are some nightmares from which there is no waking." In an evening news clip[14] NAJC president Art Miki remarked, "Today is a historic landmark, not only for our community but for the whole human rights issue." And redress campaign activist Charles Kadota reacted by stating, "The redress issue was not an issue of money; it was an issue of justice, of human rights, of citizenship."

• • •

Following the murder of George Floyd in May 2020, race riots and protests south of the Canadian border triggered memories and reminded me of images from Hirabayashi's poignant butoh performance. I asked members of my family if anyone remembered the show. No one had any recollection. Undeterred, I rifled through my community files and found the CentreStage program and *Rage* ticket stub, which read, "Kokoro Dance with the Uzume Taiko Drummers performance in the Jack Singer Concert Hall on Oct. 7, 1989." Flipping through the booklet, I noticed page after page featured Calgary-based venues, and it occurred to me the presentation was one of the main highlights during the NAJC Seniors Conference in Calgary. I had just started at the *Nikkei Voice* and was there on one of my first assignments. I remember being surrounded by JCs and the event bustling with energy; buoyed by the successes of the redress movement, the promise of inclusivity, and efforts to eliminate discrimination, it was a time when hope and optimism emerged.

By exposing the Japanese incarceration experience to a broader Canadian audience, Kokoro Dance created awareness and enriched activism efforts during the height of the redress movement. For older JCs in attendance who had been imprisoned, the productions were a reminder of past injustices. Butoh's stark imagery depicted their oppression and struggles, laid bare and raw for all to see. Devoid of dialogue, the dance captured our feelings of frustration, helplessness, and anger. In the Japanese way, it spoke to us on a deep personal level and continued to resonate long after the show ended. I was unaware of it at the time, but like a dark omen, the dance foreshadowed an undercurrent of what lay ahead for me in the years to come.

Fresh out of the radio and television program at Ryerson (now known as Toronto Metropolitan University) in early May 1989, I had to say no to a coveted position on a TV series about high school students. Though pleased to be offered the job after a successful interview, my spirits deflated when I learned the contract included no salary or benefits. It didn't matter how much previous experience I had. There were no exceptions.

"How do they expect you to work and not pay you?" Grandma asked in disbelief when I shared my dilemma. "What kind of business are they running?" Years of working in the dry cleaning business and serving customers helped shape Grandma into a shrewd businesswoman and advisor. Living under one roof, everyone in the family contributed to the household. We learned from her example of how to be practical, to stretch and save our meagre dollars.

Before I'd even heard the term "gig economy," I thought it commonplace to work more than one job at a time. Kids like us had paper routes, did odd jobs, and worked in retail or food services. We never dared to ask for handouts. Our parents were straining to make ends meet and lacked extra cash for allowances or free time to go on school field trips like the white moms. No one waited at home for us with a hot lunch or ready to bake cookies and serve after-school snacks. We had our own house keys. We learned to fend for ourselves and found jobs early on because we understood if we wanted money, we had to earn it. These necessities became a study in scheduling and time management.

After years of juggling part-time jobs and managing my own expenses, including university tuition, how in good conscience could I expect Mom to foot the bill now? I had debts to pay. I lived at home, but my sister was still away at school and Mom had her hands full with Dee's tuition fees and other household expenses. It wouldn't be right to add to her burden. Unlike my wealthy white schoolmate, who ended up taking the unpaid position, I didn't feel I could afford the luxury of an internship. Perhaps my own pride got in the way. Over the years I often wondered if I made the right decision: *How different my life might have been if only I had taken that job.*

A couple of months after graduating and still looking for work, I'd been invited to an impromptu job interview. I was intrigued from the moment I saw the job posting in *Nikkei Voice* and liked the prospect of working for a national newspaper. After all, I already had some familiarity with community news from my work as the JCCC newsletter editor. *Why not?* I thought. I may as well give it a shot. Wanting to make a positive first impression, I enlisted my mother and her friend as image consultants, and we finally settled on a vintage gingham sundress and cable-knit sweater. The pale-pink outfit presented an agreeable feminine front and softened the sharp edges.

Walking along the west end of Bloor Street, I passed Christie Pits before turning down a quiet tree-lined residential street, half expecting to find a grand dwelling. With my stomach in knots and heart pounding, I knocked at the modest semi, thinking the door would be answered by famed writer Joy Kogawa. After I was ushered in without formality, excitement quickly turned to alarm when I learned she had fallen ill and gone to the hospital. At the casual get-together, I met several Toronto NAJC members from the editorial collective as well as the favoured candidate, Byron. Confidently, he confided he had no intention of taking the position — he knew he'd find a more attractive offer elsewhere.

My tenure as managing editor began with *Nikkei Voice*'s September 1989 issue and earned me many distinctions: the first paid, the youngest, and the first biracial yonsei (fourth generation) staffer. On the first day of work, I exited the Queen Street streetcar at Spadina and walked north past a mishmash of shops from furriers to Chinese restaurants and markets, briefcase in hand. Arriving at 192 Spadina Avenue, I double-checked the address, confused at first by the prominent Perfect

Leather Goods storefront display, a long-time business fixture at street level.

Nikkei Voice shared its fourth-floor office with the Toronto NAJC. As I entered the drab hall, a door opened into a series of relatively large rooms. Secretary Blanche Hyodo presided over the lobby at her imposing central desk. On the left were two offices: Toronto NAJC president Harry Yonekura occupied the first office and *Nikkei Voice* had the second one, in the back beside the common area where meetings were held. Our office had two large metal worktables pressed together — one for me and the other for Yusuke, the Japanese section editor. Behind me huge windows boasted a skyline view overlooking Chinatown and framed strewn garbage blowing past the gritty storefronts sandwiched between run-down warehouse buildings. Tucked into a corner of the sizeable meeting room was a small wooden desk revered and rumoured to be the desk where Kogawa wrote her award-winning novel *Obasan*. While I never saw her at the office, she remained an editorial advisor and part of the collective, although many years passed before I had the chance to converse with her by email.

No longer a newsletter, *Nikkei Voice* produced ten issues per year and circulation hovered around sixteen thousand copies per issue. Volunteer editor Ken Kishibe oversaw early editions, followed by Jennifer Hashimoto, who spent long hours training me to navigate the labour-intensive printing and production process. Community supporter M. Wesley "Wes" Fujiwara, a former pediatrician, had retired and moved back to British Columbia. From there he acted as the newspaper's publisher, but due to the distance and time difference, Fujiwara remained mostly uninvolved in daily operations. Although he impressed me as a kind, grandfatherly gentleman in our phone conversations, I never met my boss face to face.

The dozen or so members of the editorial collective and three-person advisory board comprised mostly older JCs active in the fight for redress. Right away we were on different pages. I was more interested in the arts and cultural events and lacked the knowledge and history my politically minded colleagues possessed. We clashed over my desire to implement changes and their steadfast resolve to maintain the status quo. Everyone wanted to be the editor, or at least that's how it appeared to me.

I remember thinking meetings peculiar. Members enjoyed passing around submissions and making corrections on the page before fishing in a central pile for another one of the handwritten or typed articles people mailed to the office. Once finalized these articles were sent en masse to the printer, who prepared what we called van dykes. The printer returned large rolls of waxed text and photos to us for the physical cut-and-paste stage, where we manually assembled each issue by hand on preformatted typesetting boards. In contrast the JCCC's newsletter production had a streamlined method of desktop publishing: all articles were compiled, typed, and edited using a basic word processor. Once the issue was complete, I'd copy the main file onto a hard disk for delivery to the printer. Naturally, I advocated for a similar process.

Luckily, *Nikkei Voice* owned a computer for maintaining the mailing list and performing other administrative tasks. Retyping submissions dramatically reduced our printing turnaround time and costs. It also eliminated the back-and-forth corrections characterized by the earlier process. Unfamiliar with these methods, no one from the editorial collective stepped forward to volunteer their time to help with the typing. Much later on I heard from my successor, David Ikeda, how our printer was thrilled to no longer have to navigate the medley of pages and make sense of handwritten corrections.

While settling in at the paper, a chance job interview at Citytv in October 1989 went so well I was hired on the spot as the newsroom floor director. *This is what I studied for in school. Here's a great opportunity*, I thought. I didn't hesitate in accepting the position. With unprecedented media access to stories and information, I imagined myself building a career reporting on relevant community events of the day and expanding the newspaper. Young and idealistic, my illusions soon fell short. Instilled with notions of fairness and honesty, I wanted to believe if I worked hard, I'd be acknowledged and appreciated. To this day I still hold these principles and habitually strive to do my best — it's the only work ethic I know. Invariably, this overzealousness betrayed me, time and time again, at every pivotal juncture in my career.

Members from the editorial collective and advisory board started to hold evening meetings without me. On the occasions when the evening news was pushed back to eleven o'clock, I'd race over to the *Nikkei Voice* office after the six-o'clock news, wolf down something to eat during the meeting, and then leave early to make it back to the station in time for the broadcast. In trying to navigate these uncertain waters, I suggested we change meeting times to weekends or during the day; this idea fell into an abyss. From the sidelines there were whispers: *She should quit that other job.* I lacked allies, friends, or supports. My straightforward, take-charge demeanour had no influence except to alienate everyone. I had much to learn about advocating for myself. With no one to confide in, resentments took root. I felt reigned in, dictated to, and restricted.

For a time I continued diligently with two full-time jobs plus the monthly JCCC newsletter. My sense of independence and the need for self-sufficiency empowered me to attack each new goal with determination and discipline. Coffee in hand, I'd head to my Spadina office in the morning and then hop on the Queen Street streetcar to make it to John Street in time for the two o'clock lineup meeting in the newsroom. Eventually, my stamina wore thin and I preferred to sleep in after late nights at the station. Weekends spent alone in the office at the small computer station, eyes glued to the massive monitor's tiny screen, I pounded away at that keyboard. Anger and cynicism crept in. I imagined myself as a prancing marionette, a powerless pawn, unable to engage as others pulled the strings. *How the hell did I get here?* I wondered. Unable to see any options, days before my three-month probation period with the paper ended, I hastily wrote and faxed my resignation to my boss, Wes.

· · ·

Karma has many lessons to teach us. Some people regard it as a romantic notion: being bound to another soul across time and space and returning to each other during multiple lifetimes. For others it's viewed as a nightmare of antagonism where polar opposites continue to be thrust together until those bonds are eventually released or broken through acceptance and forgiveness.

There have been many times I've been caught in a continuous cycle where I return to the beginning and start over again: I charge in, overcompensate, apologize, bristle against authority. Repeat. If I could just toe the line like a good little girl, maybe I'd come out on top. Instead, I choreographed my own odori, one that saw me spiralling away from the community and then back again in an ongoing chorus. And following my lead mere steps behind, my steady dance partner continued to shadow me. I could always count on conflict.

Why couldn't I learn my lesson the first time and move on? No, I had to learn things the hard way. Maybe I had a chip on my shoulder. Maybe I wasn't ready to let things go. Impulsive and reckless at times, I'd speed through circumstances without thinking, as if life were a race. Afterward I'd rue, thinking it might have been better to carefully plan or strategize before bulldozing forward. If only I'd taken the time to reflect and gain clarity.

Years later I clued into the twelve laws of karma — those ancient Hindu and Buddhist lessons including cause and effect, the here and now, and patience and reward.[15] Behind the scenes these karmic cycles are forever at work in our lives whether we're aware of them or not. In hindsight the law of change seems so crystal clear: history will continue to repeat itself until we learn what we need to and change our path.

Grandma liked to remind us to behave ourselves wherever we went. "You never know who's watching. You don't know who knows who. Someone is always watching," she often said. I think she must have known instinctively about the law of connection — the idea that our past, present, and future are all connected. I've never asked if she'd heard about the six degrees of separation theory. Like the karmic law, it's the idea that everyone on the planet is six or fewer connections away from any other person. Thanks to social media, this number may be even smaller. And in the JC community, I invariably discover links with just about every JC I meet.

This sense of close interrelatedness provides a warm reassuring welcome, an immediate unspoken understanding.

When you are stuck in a well-worn groove of tradition and routine, this old recording makes it easy to fall into step. Within these comforting confines, where everyone and everything seems familiar, there lurks a rigidity, an expectation of conformity. Whether it's fear or contempt, any insider can quickly become an outsider should they stray from convention. Acceptance rapidly shifts to disdain. In my free-spirited youth, as the family's black sheep, I sought freedom and independence, but early on, I discovered the chains stretch only so far and you're yanked back by shackles before you make it beyond the enclosure.

Turning my back on the chummy circles and same old songs, years passed while I distanced myself from the community. Yet a nagging sense of unfinished business persisted. One afternoon, at the Buddhist temple for the funeral of one of my great-uncles, I ran into long-time *Nikkei Voice* columnist Frank Moritsugu. He'd become the publisher during my absence. The current managing editor, Jesse Nishihata, needed to retire. The former filmmaker, educator, and author had begun his battle with Alzheimer's. Frank needed to find a replacement. Would I consider returning to my former post?

Mulling things over, I felt my wings had been clipped before I was able to launch. I wanted to set things right, and second chances rarely present themselves. After a decade in television, the thought of returning to print intrigued me. Plus I'd been thrown off balance by an unexpected layoff. My quick ascent to management hadn't prepared me for the possibility of suddenly being "mommy-tracked" from the CBC in June 2000. And despite rebounding as the part-time administrator at Japanese Social Services, my desire to regain my footing in media remained.

Frank's timing struck me as auspicious. Western astrology divides every year into twelve zodiac signs, whereas in the Chinese zodiac, each year is represented by one of twelve different animals. A twelve-year period had passed, completing a full cycle, and it was the year of the Horse. Having been born under that sign, I thought, *This is my year, it should be filled with lucky breaks, right?* Unfortunately, I didn't know about *ben ming jian*.[16] According to Chinese folklore, birth years are unlucky. The presiding wisdom stresses avoiding obstacles and adversity by using caution: lay low and avoid changing jobs or making any major life changes. Oblivious to all of this, in February 2002 I reprised my role; by the March issue, I had stepped back into the familiar rhythm, ready to finish what I had started.

Nikkei Voice had relocated to the second floor of the new JCCC building on Garamond Court. Independent from the NAJC, it now relied on paid subscriptions. A board of directors had replaced both the editorial collective and advisory board. Frank did double duty as publisher and columnist, and he tried to guide me as best he could on running the paper. The former teacher, Canadian Army sergeant, accomplished journalist, and *judoka* was a few years younger than my grandmother. He probably expected more respect from his juniors and never thought he'd be challenged. He balked if changes or corrections needed to be made to his column, however slight. We butted heads. His lovely wife, Betty, the steadfast voice of reason, sometimes stepped in to act as intermediary.

Our printer had petitioned the paper for years to update our methods and was happy to finally find a receptive ear. He advocated for the more economically sound process of emailing page layouts as PDFs rather than driving the computer disk out to the printing factory on Eastern Avenue. With my reinstatement as managing editor, I quickly incorporated this technology and began to send files electronically. The editor of the Japanese section, Yusuke, remained the constant amid these changes. He had married the daughter of one of my neighbours from Greektown and had a family. I think he'd grown used to calling the shots during Jesse's decline and resented my return. Outgoing and animated one moment, he'd burst into sudden furious tirades if I mentioned the stylistic conventions of mainstream publications or pointed out typos in his English captions. It offended my sense of office decorum to see him padding around in stocking feet on the dingy carpet or casually eating ramen and amassing food items on his bookshelf. He never confided in me, but I later heard he divorced. In hindsight my stringent attitude toward our work schedules probably only aggravated the situation.

Seldom did a day pass when our aging Apple computer didn't crash; it barely contained enough memory to produce one issue let alone store back issues digitally. My routine included rebooting and deleting unnecessary files. Our issues, printed on flimsy newsprint, were disintegrating, making referencing old articles difficult. Wanting to create a virtual library and database of past articles, I typed up a business case for a new computer and website. Frank and I were soon at an impasse. Why spend money on an upgrade? Our computer works fine, he argued. What do we need a website for? As old roadblocks lifted, new hurdles remained. For the next five years, Frank and I continued to disagree over how things should be managed. Signing off on the December 2004 issue at the end of the year, I'd had enough and decided, *It's time to resign. I'm ready to move on.*

Twelve years rolled by, completing another cycle of the Chinese zodiac and leaving my youth behind. While I was at the JCCC in February 2017, *Nikkei Voice* board member Marty Kobayashi saw me leafing through a copy of the paper. Paid subscriptions had fallen to sixteen hundred by 2015 and the publication was on the cusp of folding. With my knowledge and years of experience working in publishing, Marty asked if I would consider attending a board strategy meeting on his behalf and share any insights. I went with an open mind. Midway through the meeting, the current publisher resigned and asked if I would assume the role. Taken aback I hesitated. No longer one to rush in, I had learned to survey the environment before charging ahead and getting caught in the mire. I'd been burned too many times before and had learned to temper both ire and enthusiasm with age. Was it indifference, apathy, or simply exhaustion? Truth be told, I was tired of fighting, tired of waiting to be seen and heard, and tired of waiting for my turn, my seat at the table.

Nikkei Voice finally launched a website, but with limited archives dating back to November 2012 it was not what I envisioned many years ago. Still there was so much potential to turn things around. Surrounded by about a dozen well-meaning board members, I made several suggestions: consider a digital edition, build a social media platform, increase website content. Judging by their blank stares, these methods were unknown to them, and my ideas evaporated into cyberspace. Thinking back I realize JCs are often hesitant to speak out if they don't understand something. Even within my family of strong matriarchs, I've noticed relatives who are quite vocal on the home front suddenly switch to the defensive or become quiet and afraid to speak in the outside world. Perhaps we never learned how to respond appropriately and, instead, lash out at those who are closest to us. Somehow, it's easier to fight amongst ourselves rather than confront the larger establishment responsible for our sense of disenfranchisement.

Certainly, JCs are traditionally reserved and cautious to begin with. According to Ruth Ozeki, Japanese Americans are no different: "I suspect all families have this, some code of silence that is absolute and inviolable and yet so omnipresent as to be almost invisible, too."[17] Depending on the generation, combine these factors with trauma, strict parents, discrimination, and anxiety, and suddenly, we're a silent self-conscious society. Somewhere along the line, JCs were led to believe that asking questions makes them look foolish. Saving face is more important.

Following the meeting, I spoke briefly with a couple of the attendees whom I immediately pegged as biracial. Each member took a moment to explain what it meant to be "mixed" and how they each had one Japanese parent. Several thoughts flashed through my mind: *Why did they feel the need to tell me this? Don't they see I'm Japanese, too? Do I really look that white to them? Had these people become accustomed to explaining why they looked the way they did? Or was it the need to justify their involvement in cultural affairs because they weren't entirely Japanese?* Perhaps they just didn't see me as one of them.

Afterward, I tried to help by sending heaps of information with links to funding sources, digital hosts, and publishing trends. My name appeared as a board member on the masthead and then quickly vanished. I don't know what I did or said, but after attending another meeting or two, no further invitations were issued. I imagine my name was erased from the email distribution lists. Clearly, I still hadn't learned to get along with others. Maybe, as JCs, we're not the model minority others believe us to be. Rather than perpetuate any myths, maybe we mirror our own dysfunctional relationships with uncanny precision.

Outside of family, will I ever find my clan? Not that I'm looking for a specific group of Japanese Germans (although I'm sure there's enough of us out there) but simply a connection with a group of like-minded individuals. In the eyes of elders like my grandmother, I'm one of the young people and the journey, if we're lucky, is long. More than half a century has passed, but I'm still a child at heart searching for a place of belonging where I don't have to define my identity by fractions of ethnicity. What part is Japanese, German, or Canadian? Our lives are more than the sum of our DNA. Yet to be biracial is to be tethered to the undertones both vague and specific: two entirely different faces on one coin.

I'm reminded of the butoh scene — the more I tried to push forward, the more I was held back, bound in a continuous cycle of ebb and flow. How is it possible to hold contrasting views at the same time? Is there a way to harmonize these polarized viewpoints? How can I be all these identities and none of them? It's been a lifetime of struggle in this ongoing journey to find acceptance and inner peace.

Growing up in two worlds, two cultures, and with two sets of values, many JCs were raised with conflicting ideals, which we failed to reconcile. This combative duality clouded our perceptions. On the one hand, we'd been built up with the promise of the North American dream; we earnestly pushed ahead and worked hard for recognition and rewards, like the squeaky wheel that gets the grease, yet somehow these dreams of merit often failed to materialize and never harmonized when held to Japanese standards. Conformity cajoled us to keep quiet, to not make trouble, to stay in the shadows. I'd been warned many times, *the nail that sticks out gets hammered in.*

. . .

During the Covid-19 pandemic, the daily news featured a surge of disturbing images as anti-Asian sentiments spread across the country. Toward the end of April 2020, an older Asian man in Vancouver was grabbed by a hulking white man who tossed him like a rag doll out of a store onto the concrete, where he fell and hit his head. Less than two weeks later, a young Asian woman was waiting for the bus when a white passerby suddenly turned and punched her in the face. A Filipino woman broke down in tears while she recollected riding the Toronto subway when a man struck her and launched into a verbal assault, yelling "Go back to China." Montreal temples were desecrated. Increased incidents of vandalism, discrimination, and anti-Asian acts prompted the creation of covidracism.ca, a website spearheaded by the Asian community to monitor and tally racism.

On June 3, 2020, British Columbia premier John Horgan called for an antiracism program and urged the federal government to act. He specifically named Chinese Canadians, South Asians, and Indigenous Peoples as having "experienced racism from the beginning of settlement here in British Columbia."[18] Somehow the dispossession and incarceration of JCs slipped his mind. Horgan's exclusion didn't escape the attention of offended JCs. The Toronto NAJC called the premier's omission stunning on its website: "Selective amnesia is a type of systemic racism, a step towards the erasure of a community's history."[19]

Deemed an enemy by the Canadian government during the Second World War, we were vilified, reviled, and shamed for our culture, our heritage, and our language. Ripped from homes, lives torn apart, and remnants thrown to the wind, the JC community was pounded down and deliberately shattered. How does one recover from that? We may be considered fractured but we are still one. Through increased intermarriage, many of our key ethnic markers have faded and diluted the visible threat we once were. Robbed of our birthright and at the edge of erasure generations later, an ambiguous identity has become our inheritance.

The more I learn about our history, the more I'm struck by the resilience of the JC community and its immense contributions to the Canadian landscape. And despite the inhospitable soil, the community persisted and refused to die. Where do we go from here? Is there a clear path shining the way forward? Maybe the answer to our future survival lies deep within our ancestral culture. If we return to our roots, we may find the salve.

There's an ancient art of repairing Japanese pottery known as *kintsugi*, which uses a special lacquer mixed with gold, silver, or platinum as an adhesive. Instead of trying to camouflage or hide the cracks, artists refashion the mended piece into a stronger, more striking, one-of-a-kind work. With this technique, nothing is ever wasted and the unique history and artistry continues to be celebrated in all its imperfections and visible scars. *Kintsugi* incorporates long-held Japanese ideas many JCs inherently know and recognize. We've absorbed through osmosis these intrinsic concepts, many of which originate from Buddhist philosophies, which celebrate the natural world and our limited time in it. Notions of *wabi-sabi*, or beautiful imperfections, are themes running through many Japanese artistic practices from *sumi-e* to *ikebana*. *Mottainai* encompasses the idea we should avoid wastefulness and fix or reuse items. In this regard our issei and nisei can be viewed as recycling pioneers. As for *mushin*, this idea of slowing down and emptying your mind into a meditative state is harder to translate and is often considered a way of accepting change.[20]

There is a darkness within. It's part of who I am, who I've become, who I've always been. I stumbled on the existence of this inner shadow after breaking my leg in a freak accident and while recovering from knee surgery. Confined to bed and unable to walk, I was overcome with feelings of helplessness, which awakened something, an unsettling awareness. The physical pain from reassembling my shattered bones forced a surge of hidden emotions to surface. Falling into an abyss, I grew restless, drowning in agitation. My head flailed back and forth as I floundered in this stagnant air, in a frenzied effort to remain afloat. Scanning my surroundings, I blindly searched for any passage to ferry me out of that moment. My captive mind continued to race ahead, but I was trapped in the busted shell of my own body. Like the restrained butoh dancer who was unable to move, I struggled through this paralysis, day to day, minute by minute. In my desperation to regain mobility, a deep overwhelming tide rushed in and engulfed me. I was struck with keen insight: *We are all broken.*

Is there hope beyond this despair? Are we ready to close the curtain on our fury? Can we reforge those links to lost traditions and teachings? How do we find our voice and words unknown? Will we devise a way to recast and transform?

In an effort to heal these wounds and regain status, pride, and battered self-esteem, we're piecing together the stolen and discarded segments of generations of former lives. By mining the dark passages, we unearth snippets of light: a patchwork kimono, isolated lyrics in a forgotten song, a dance forever etched in memory. Each measured step is an illuminating glimpse, a momentary floodlight on what has been obscured from view. In this slow-moving choreography, we're staging a whole new production by carefully gathering and reassembling the broken bits, these beautiful fragments.

ACKNOWLEDGEMENTS

THANK YOU TO all my literary partners (with apologies to anyone I may have missed) for sharing my work with a wider audience. To the team at Dundurn Press: publisher Meghan Macdonald and COO Chris Houston; project editor Erin Pinksen; art director Laura Boyle for the striking cover and interior design; and especially acquiring editor Julia Kim, who understood and championed the project from day one.

Produced with the support of the City of Toronto through the Toronto Arts Council, this book would not have been possible without the support of my husband, Gaëtan Belair, and the continued urging of our child, Camille Kiku Belair.

To Grandma, Mom, and Dee for answering endless questions and sharing their stories. And the extended Nakamura and Goto family members for their patience during the process: Aunts Marlene, Norma, Judy, Sakae, and Tomo; Uncles George and Tin; and cousins Alana, Paul, Pam, Eleanor, Yoshimi, Sanae, and Stan.

To my godparents, Carole and Sam Cooper, for their ongoing support, even when they were no longer with us.

At the University of King's College, Kim Pittaway and Stephen Kimber urged me to get this book out of my head and onto paper during the MFA program. With special thanks to my King's mentors, Lorri Neilsen Glenn and Ken McGoogan, who read early drafts, offered encouragement, and made great suggestions. Fellow students in the King's history chicks writers group (Susan Rhodemyre Willmot, Wendy Elliott, Sarah Toye, and Kirsten Fogg) helped me clarify much of the writing, as did the GES Writers Trio (Gloria Blizzard and Elida Schogt).

The Writer's Union of Canada hosted the inspiring BIPOC Writer's Connect event, and mentor Sally Ito provided feedback on the Miss Tokyo chapter. Thanks to Mata Ashita Japanese Canadian writer's circle for printing an excerpt of that chapter and to the Draft Reading Series Mixed Tongues season for the opportunity to read from the work in progress.

To the many community organizations and members who helped with my research and provided resources: the National Association of Japanese Canadians (NAJC) for funding my early research, with thanks to Lynn Deutscher Kobayashi (Toronto NAJC) for supporting my application; Pamela Yoshida and Amy Wakisaka at Toronto Buddhist Church; Rev. Joan Wilson and Lynne Nagata at St. Andrew's Japanese Congregation; Joyce Nakagawa at Toronto Japanese Language School; community members Michiko Yano-Shuttleworth, Debbie Suyama Katsumi, Mark Nishihama; and writers Kerri Sakamoto, Terry Watada, Raymond Nakamura, Leanne Toshiko Simpson, Andrea Sakiyama Kennedy, Lara Okihiro, and Yukari Peerless. Arigato gozaimasu.

NOTES

1 Mukashi, Mukashi

1 Yasuko Nishimura letter to Shigeru Nakamura, University of Toronto, East Asian Studies, March 1982.
2 On Sengoku.com, the Satake family is listed as descendants of eleventh-century warrior Yoshimitsu Minamoto. The Minamoto name is attributed to former members of the imperial family who were excluded from succession lines and demoted from the nobility. The Satake crest of a rising sun with five bones features an open foldable fan and is believed to have been designed in the twelfth century.
3 John Tory, "Japanese Canadian Freedom Day," Facebook, April 1, 2021, facebook.com/photo/?fbid=10165350969310495 &set=a.10150175732745495.

2 The Kimono

1 *Japanese Merchant Ships Recognition Handbook*, maritime.org /doc/id/oni208j-japan-merchant-ships/front003.htm.
2 Julie Otsuka, *The Buddha in the Attic* (Farmington Hills, MI: Thorndike Press, 1995), 12.
3 Ken Adachi, *The Enemy That Never Was* (Toronto: McClelland & Stewart, 1991), 87–94.
4 Adachi, *The Enemy That Never Was*, 87–92.
5 Margery Hadley, "Oriental Home and School Photos Online," Pacific Mountain Regional Council of The United Church of Canada, April 16, 2016, pacificmountain.ca/oriental -home-and-school-photos-online/.

4 First to the Horse Stalls

1   Japanese Canadian Cultural Centre Archives, "Life in the Canadian Internment and POW Camps," Discover Nikkei, discovernikkei.org/en/nikkeialbum/albums/6/slide/?page=2.

2   Toyo Takata, *Nikkei Legacy: The Story of Japanese Canadians from Settlement to Today* (Toronto: New Canada Publications, 1983), 139.

3   "Buildings," Hastings Park 1942, accessed January 16, 2020, hastingspark1942.ca/buildings-overview/livestock-building/.

4   Takata, *Nikkei Legacy*, 120.

5   "Buildings," Hastings Park 1942.

6   Michael S. Hoshiko, *Who Was Who: Pioneer Japanese Families in Delta and Surrey* (Marceline, MO: Herff Jones, 1998), 6.

7   Takata, *Nikkei Legacy*, 137.

8   JCs with cognitive issues like Yasukichi were essentially locked up and held indefinitely at Essondale. In 2014 the kʷikʷəƛ̓əm (Kwikwetlem First Nation) made a traditional territory claim on the Riverview Lands and is restoring the grounds as a place of healing. səmiq̓ʷəʔelə Place of the Great Blue Heron, sumiqwuelu.com/home.

9   Hoshiko, *Who Was Who*, 6–9.

10   Takata, *Nikkei Legacy*, 142.

11   Janet McLellan, *Many Petals of the Lotus: Five Asian Buddhist Communities in Toronto* (Toronto: University of Toronto Press, 1999), 50.

5 The Church Buddhists Built

1   Terry Watada, *Bukkyo Tozen: A History of Jodo Shinshu Buddhism in Canada 1905–1995* (Toronto: Toronto Buddhist Church, 1996), 97, 297–99.

2   John S. Harding, Victor Sōgen Hori, and Alexander Soucy, *Wild Geese: Buddhism in Canada* (Montreal/Kingston: McGill-Queen's University Press, 2010), 4–7.

3   "About BCA," Buddhist Churches of America, buddhistchurchesofamerica.org/bca-history/.

4   "Buddhism in Canada," Jodo Shinshu Buddhist Temples of Canada, jsbtc.ca/jodoshinshu/history.html.

5   Watada, *Bukkyo Tozen,* 145-47, 261.

6   Mark R. Mullins, "The Organizational Dilemmas of Ethnic Churches: A Case Study of Japanese Buddhism in Canada," *Sociology of Religion* 49, no. 3 (Fall 1988): 217–33.

7   McLellan, *Many Petals of the Lotus,* 35.

8   Amy Wakisaka, email interview with the author, November 1, 2019.

9   McLellan, *Many Petals of the Lotus,* 25.

10 Susan Reid, "Congregation Fights Sale of Church," *Toronto Star,* June 24, 1991, Ontario edition, A20.

11 Marites "Tess" Sison, "Japan Trip Highlights Canadian Connections," *Anglican Journal,* September 11, 2012, accessed October 28, 2019, anglican.ca/news/japan-trip-highlights-canadian-connections/300466/.

12 Rev. Joan Wilson, email interview with the author, October 28, 2019.

13 "About," Toronto Creative Music Lab, tcml-admin.squarespace.com/.

14 Maryka Omatsu, *Swimming Upstream: Japanese Canadian Struggle for Justice in BC* (The Canadian Race Relations Foundation, 2018).

15 "BC Redress," NAJC, accessed October 25, 2019, bcredress.ca/.

16 "About Japanese Canadian BC Redress," *The Bulletin,* November 2019, 7.

17 Nicholas Keung, "Buddhist Church Rejoices; Parishioners Succeed in Preserving Their Heritage While Integrating into Canadian Society Modern New House of Worship, Opening Today, Testament to 60-Year Effort," *Toronto Star,* August 20, 2005, Ontario edition, A13.

18 Keung, "Buddhist Church Rejoices," A13.

6 A Time to Remember

1   Despite searching, I hadn't been able to determine the author of this Japanese tanka poem. Although the translation varies for "The Cry of the Crane," thanks to proofreader Tim Hilts at Dundurn, two works containing the poem were discovered. Both listed the author as Ki no Tsurayuki. Stephen Addiss, *The Art of Haiku: Its History Through Poems and Paintings* by Japanese Masters (Boston: Shambhala Publications, 2012), 30; and Kenneth Rexroth, *One Hundred Poems from the Japanese* (New York: New Directions, 1955), 86.
2   Mock Joya, *Quaint Customs and Manners of Japan*, vols. 1 & 2 (Tokyo: Tokyo News Service, 1951), 149–51.
3   "Obon," Toronto Buddhist Church, tbc.on.ca/join-us/special-observances-services/.
4   Eric M. Adams, "How Japanese Canadians Shaped the Constitution" (lecture, University of Toronto, Toronto, ON, November 7, 2019).
5   Adachi, *The Enemy That Never Was*, 72–74.
6   Adachi, *The Enemy That Never Was*, 81–85.
7   McLellan, *Many Petals of the Lotus*, 45.
8   Harding et al., *Wild Geese*, 70.
9   Watada, *Bukkyo Tozen*, 326–28.
10   Adams, "How Japanese Canadians Shaped the Constitution."
11   Watada, *Bukkyo Tozen*, 313-25.
12   Harding et al., *Wild Geese*, 4, 26–27.
13   Toronto Buddhist Church, "A Jodo Shinshu Temple Located in Toronto," accessed September 17, 2019, tbc.on.ca/.

7 Heart and Soul

1   Macy DuBois, *Japanese Canadian Cultural Centre: An Appraisal* (Toronto: Japanese Canadian Cultural Centre, 1963). Reprinted from *The Canadian Architect*, March 1964, Marlene MacKenzie collection.

2   Japanese Canadian Cultural Centre, *Official Opening of the Japanese Canadian Cultural Centre by The Right Honourable Lester B. Pearson Prime Minister of Canada* (Toronto: Japanese Canadian Cultural Centre, Toronto, ON, 1964), Marlene MacKenzie collection.

3   "Sansei Choir Seeks More New Members," *Continental Times*, October 11, 1966, Mark Nishihama collection.

4   Mark Nishihama, email interviews with the author, July 7–October 30, 2020.

5   Ken Mori, "J.C. Centennial Committee Approved 'Canada Ondo' Recording Now on Sale," *New Canadian*, June 3, 1967, Mark Nishihama collection.

6   "Obon Odori Attracts Best Crowd Ever," *Continental Times*, July 14, 1967, Mark Nishihama collection.

7   "The Building," Noor Cultural Centre, noorculturalcentre.ca/about-2/the-building/.

8 Odori Primer

1   Jon Wertheim, "Kabuki: Inside the Japanese Artform with Its Biggest Star, Ebizo," *60 Minutes*, April 19, 2020, CBS News, cbsnews.com/news/kabuki-japanese-theater-art-make-up-dances-ebizo-60-minutes-2020-04-19/.

2   Noboru Fukushima, "The Discourse of Representation — Focusing on Onnagata Actors in Shakespeare's Plays," June 2006, cit.nihon-u.ac.jp/laboratorydata/kenkyu/publication/journal_b/b39.2.pdf; Laura Payne, "Izumo no Okuni: The Woman Who Created Kabuki," *GaijinPot* (blog), June 12, 2023, blog.gaijinpot.com/izumo-no-okuni-the-woman-who-created-kabuki/.

3   George Nakamura confirmed the Yamashita details and remembered Masao's last name was different.

4   Gabe Bergado, "The History of Yellowface," *Teen Vogue*, May 17, 2019, YouTube video, 6:39, youtube.com/watch?v=v3GUy25_uhE.

5   Josephine Lee, *The Japan of Pure Invention: Gilbert & Sullivan's* The Mikado (Minneapolis: University of Minnesota Press, 2010), 57.
6   Lee, *The Japan of Pure Invention*, 66, 167.
7   Josephine Lee, "Yellowface Performance: Historical and Contemporary Contexts," *Oxford Research Encyclopedia of Literature*, February 25, 2019, accessed August 11, 2020, oxfordre.com/literature/display/10.1093/acrefore/9780190201098.001.0001/acrefore-9780190201098-e-834.
8   "Alderman Ying Hope Thinks 'The Nutcracker' Is Racist, and ..." UPI, January 2, 1981, upi.com/Archives/1981/01/02/Alderman-Ying-Hope-thinks-The-Nutcracker-is-racist-and/4799347259600/.
9   "About Us," Final Bow for Yellowface, yellowface.org.
10 Michael Brooke, "The Hays Code," Screenonline, screenonline.org.uk/film/id/592022/.
11 Lisa Richwine, "Study Finds Asians Largely 'Invisible' in Hollywood's Top Films," Reuters, May 19, 2021, reuters.com/lifestyle/study-finds-asians-largely-invisible-hollywoods-top-films-2021-05-18/.
12 Bruce Demara, "Simu Liu Calls Out Producers of 'Kim's Convenience' on Facebook," *Toronto Star*, June 6, 2021, A19.

9 Miss Tokyo

1   Ruth Ozeki, *The Face: A Time Code* (Amherst, MA: Restless Books, 2015), 94.
2   Victoria Sherrow, *Encyclopedia of Hair: A Cultural History* (Westport, CT: Greenwood Press, 2006), 221.
3   Sherrow, *Encyclopedia of Hair*, 223.
4   Ozeki, *The Face*, 106–7.
5   Community Folk Art Council, *Nationbulders '67 Folk Festival* (Toronto: Community Folk Art Council, 1967), Marlene MacKenzie collection.

6   Noor Javed, "The Couple Who Put Toronto on the Map," *Toronto Star*, April 4, 2009, thestar.com/news/gta/the-couple -who-put-toronto-on-the-map/article_56d90c02-72a5-5856 -9556-e688aecbc828.html.

7   Japanese Canadian Cultural Centre 25th Anniversary Publication Board, *Salute to 25 Years: 1963–1988* (Toronto: Japanese Canadian Cultural Centre, 1988), 22.

8   Lisa Wallin, "Nihongami: Japanese Hairstyles Through the Ages," *Tokyo Weekender*, January 10, 2018, tokyoweekender.com/2018/01/nihongami-japanese-hairstyles -through-the-ages/.

9   Sui Sin Far, "Leaves from the Mental Portfolio of an Eurasian," Quotidiana, essays.quotidiana.org/far/leaves_mental _portfolio/.

10 Vito Adriaensens, "Winnifred Eaton," in *Women Film Pioneers Project*, ed. Jane Gaines, Radha Vatsal, and Monica Dall'Asta (New York: Columbia University Libraries, 2017), doi.org /10.7916/d8-zf18-vk03.

11 Far, "Leaves."

12 Takashi Ohki, "Demographic Characteristics of Japanese Canadians in 2016," najc.ca/wp-content/uploads/2018 /05/2016-Census-Japanese-Canadians-Eng-Final.pdf.

10 Natsu Matsuri

1   "Nisei Veterans' Award," *Japanese Canadian Cultural Centre Newsletter* 42, no. 8 (June/July 2006): 18, yumpu.com/ en/document/read/15756505/june-july-japanese-canadian -cultural-centre.

2   "Volunteer Awards," Japanese Canadian Cultural Centre, jccc.on .ca/join-support/volunteer/volunteer-awards.

3   "Bon Odori Season Approaches," *Japanese Canadian Cultural Centre Newsletter* 16, no. 5 (June/July 1990): 5.

4   "Past Trauma May Haunt Your Future Health," Harvard Health Publishing, February 12, 2021, health.harvard

.edu/diseases-and-conditions/past-trauma-may-haunt-your -future-health.

5   Pamela Sugiman, "Passing Time, Moving Memories: Interpreting Wartime Narratives of Japanese Canadian Women," *Histoire sociale/Social History* 37, no. 73 (2004): 78–79.

6   "What Is Nikkei?" Discover Nikkei, discovernikkei.org/en /about/what-is-nikkei.

7   "International Day of Nikkei," Kaigai Nikkeijin Kyokai, June 20, 2019, YouTube video, 1:39, youtube.com/watch ?v=aVaLYD8vojg&t=7s.

8   The Association of Nikkei & Japanese Abroad, "The Declaration of the 59th Convention of Nikkei & Japanese Abroad," jadesas.or.jp/jp/wp-content/uploads /2022/01/59_taikai_sengen_en.pdf.

9   "Background of the Event," Japanese Overseas Association, jadesas.or.jp/jp/taikai/.

10 Roberto Oshiro Teruya, "International Nikkei Day — June 20, 2018," trans. Kora McNaughton, Discover Nikkei, July 31, 2018, discovernikkei.org/en/journal/2018/7/31/dia -internacional-nikkei/?fbclid=IwAR2ra40DJiuBXnI69xV WhprjoYExIU7vwzf1GSX6rSANTqkaMwVJKIEnaZ8#. Xu6CNMVt64o.facebook.

11 Orde Street Revisited

1   Akiko Motoyoshi, "Understanding Written Japanese," in *Japanese Phrase Book* (London: BBC Books, 1995), 15–18.

2   Roland M. Kawano, *Ministry to the Hopelessly Hopeless: Japanese Canadian Evacuees and Churches during WWII* (Scarborough, ON: The Japanese Canadian Christian Churches Historical Project, 1997), 26–32, 42, 58.

3   Beatrice Fihn and Setsuko Thurlow, "International Campaign to Abolish Nuclear Weapons Nobel Lecture," February 11, 2021, Oslo City Hall, transcript, nobelprize.org/prizes/peace /2017/ican/lecture/.

4   Toronto Japanese Language School (TJLS), *Ayumi: Toronto Japanese Language School Fortieth Anniversary 1949–1989*, 5.

5   TJLS, *Ayumi*, 5.

6   "Welcome to the Toronto Japanese Language School," Toronto Japanese Language School, tjls.ca.

7   "Heritage, Education, and Planning: The Orde Street School Building," Orde Street School: 100 Years of History, 2015, ordestreetschool100.blogspot.com/?view=classic.

8   "Toronto Japanese Language School 60th Year," enikka1video, February 27, 2010, YouTube video, 3:51, youtube.com/watch ?v=e-Z-apsvuc0.

9   "The Legendary Singer Kyu Sakamoto Who Was Gone in a Plane Accident — Let's Walk Facing Up!" Famous & Popular Japan, December 4, 2017, famous-popular.tokyo/en/joyful /entertainment-en/song/1446/.

10 Matthew Hernon, "8 Things You Didn't Know About Kyu Sakamoto, the 'Sukiyaki' Singer Who Perished in Japan's Deadliest Plane Crash," *Tokyo Weekender*, August 12, 2020, tokyoweekender.com/2020/08/8-things-you-didnt -know-about-kyu-sakamoto-the-sukiyaki-singer-who-perished-in -japans-deadliest-plane-crash/.

11 Motoyoshi, *Japanese Phrase Book*, 15.

12 Kelly Bates, "Racial Imposter Syndrome," Interaction Institute for Social Change, October 11, 2019, interactioninstitute.org /racial-imposter-syndrome/.

13 Bates, "Racial Imposter Syndrome."

14 Bates, "Racial Imposter Syndrome."

15 Bates, "Racial Imposter Syndrome."

16 Kirsten Weir, "Feel Like a Fraud?" *GradPsych* 11, no. 4 (November 2013), apa.org/gradpsych/2013/11/fraud.

17 Millie Hall, "Racial Imposter Syndrome: Finding 'Mixed Race' Belonging Through 'Fake' Racial Identity," *NBGA*, May 5, 2019, nobasicgirlsallowed.com/racial-imposter-syndrome -finding-mixed-race-belonging-through-fake-racial-identity.

18 Maria P.P. Root, "A Bill of Rights for Racially Mixed People,"
    in *The Multiracial Experience: Racial Borders as the New
    Frontier*, ed. Maria P. P. Root (Thousand Oaks, CA: Sage,
    1996), 3–14.

12 Rage

1   Kokoro Dance Theatre Society, kokoro.ca. Sections on their
    repertoire, shows, and history have been deleted.
2   Margarett Loke, "Butoh: Dance of Darkness," *New York
    Times Magazine*, November 1, 1987, nytimes.com/1987/11/01
    /magazine/butoh-dance-of-darkness.html.
3   William Andrews, "'Butoh': The Dance of Death and
    Disease," *Japan Times*, May 28, 2016, japantimes.co.jp
    /culture/2016/05/28/books/book-reviews/butoh-dance-death
    -disease/.
4   Kokoro Dance Theatre Society, kokoro.ca. Sections on their
    repertoire and history have been deleted.
5   John Endo Greenaway, "Kokoro Dance: Heart, Soul &
    Spirit," *The Bulletin*, November 1, 2015, jccabulletin-geppo
    .ca/kokoro-dance-heart-soul-spirit/.
6   Greenaway, "Kokoro Dance."
7   *Hirabayashi v. United States*, 627 F. Supp. 1445 - Dist.
    Court, WD Washington 1986, scholar.google.ca/scholar
    _case?case=78520577775138891482&hl=en&as_sdt=6&as_vis
    =1&oi=scholarr.
8   Eury Chang with Yutian Wong, *Contemporary Directions in
    Asian American Dance* (Madison: University of Wisconsin
    Press, 2016), 98.
9   Chang with Wong, *Contemporary Directions*, 97.
10 Chang with Wong, *Contemporary Directions*, 102.
11 Tomoko Makabe, "No Easy Task Launching Nikkei Voice,"
    Nikkei Voice 16, no. 10 (December 2002–January 2003): 1, 13.
12 Makabe, "No Easy Task," 13.

13 "Government Apologizes to Japanese Canadians in 1988," CBC, September 22, 1988, cbc.ca/archives/government -apologizes-to-japanese-canadians-in-1988-1.4680546.

14 Wendy Mesley and Karen Webb, "The National with Peter Mansbridge, Government Apologizes to Japanese Canadians in 1988," CBC, September 22, 1988, CBC Archives video, 4:30, cbc.ca/archives/government-apologizes-to-japanese -canadians-in-1988-1.4680546.

15 "The 12 Laws of Karma Everyone Should Know!" Happy Buddha, beinghappybuddha.com/blogs/insights/the-12-laws -of-karma-everyone-should-know.

16 "Ben ming jian," Your Chinese Astrology, yourchineseastrology .com/zodiac/benmingnian.htm.

17 Ozeki, *The Face*, 49.

18 "B.C. Premier Addresses History of Racism in Province," Global News, June 3, 2020, Global News video, 2:14, globalnews.ca/video/7023890/b-c-premier-addresses-history -of-racism-in-province.

19 National Association of Japanese Canadians Greater Toronto Chapter, "Premier Horgan's Sin of Omission," press release, June 10, 2020, torontonajc.ca/2020/06/10/premier -horgans-sin-of-omission/.

20 Kelly Richman-Abdou, "Kintsugi: The Centuries-Old Art of Repairing Broken Pottery with Gold," My Modern Met, September 5, 2019, mymodernmet.com/kintsugi-kintsukuroi/.

BIBLIOGRAPHY

Adachi, Ken. *The Enemy That Never Was*. Toronto: McClelland & Stewart, 1991.

Adams, Eric M. "How Japanese Canadians Shaped the Constitution." Lecture presented by the Greater Toronto Chapter of National Association of Japanese Canadians at the University of Toronto, Toronto, ON, November 7, 2019.

Addiss, Stephen. *The Art of Haiku: Its History Through Poems and Paintings by Japanese Masters*. Boston: Shambhala Publications, 2012.

Adriaensens, Vito. "Winnifred Eaton." In *Women Film Pioneers Project*, edited by Jane Gaines, Radha Vatsal, and Monica Dall'Asta. New York: Columbia University Libraries, 2017. doi.org/10.7916/d8-zf18-vk03.

"Alderman Ying Hope Thinks 'The Nutcracker' Is Racist, and ..." UPI, January 2, 1981. upi.com/Archives/1981/01/02/ Alderman-Ying-Hope-thinks-The-Nutcracker-is-racist-and /4799347259600/.

Andrews, William. "'Butoh': The Dance of Death and Disease." *Japan Times*, May 28, 2016. japantimes.co.jp/culture/2016/05/28/ books/book-reviews/butoh-dance-death-disease/.

Association of Nikkei & Japanese Abroad. "The Declaration of the 59th Convention of Nikkei & Japanese Abroad." jadesas.or.jp /jp/wp-content/uploads/2022/01/59_taikai_sengen_en.pdf.

Bates, Kelly. "Racial Imposter Syndrome." Interaction Institute for Social Change, October 11, 2019. Interaction Institute for Social Change. interactioninstitute.org/racial-imposter-syndrome/.

"B.C. Premier Addresses History of Racism in Province." Global News, June 3, 2020. Global News video, 2:14. globalnews.ca /video/7023890/b-c-premier-addresses-history-of-racism-in -province.

"Ben ming jian." Your Chinese Astrology. yourchineseastrology .com/zodiac/benmingnian.htm.

Bergado, Gabe. "The History of Yellowface." Teen Vogue, May 17, 2019. YouTube video, 6:39. youtube.com /watch?v=v3GUy25_uhE.

Brooke, Michael. "The Hays Code." Screenonline. screenonline .org.uk/film/id/592022/.

Buddhist Churches of America. "About BCA." buddhistchurchesofamerica.org/bca-history/.

The Bulletin. "About Japanese Canadian BC Redress." November 2019: 7. drive.google.com/file/d/1x7G5a7IGCCocQRg-k4xx MVLjB5hALhzJ/view.

Chang, Eury Colin, with Yutian Wong. Contemporary Directions in Asian American Dance. Madison: University of Wisconsin Press, 2016.

Community Folk Art Council. Nationbuilders '67 Folk Festival. Toronto: Community Folk Art Council, 1967. From the personal collection of Marlene MacKenzie.

Demara, Bruce. "Simu Liu Calls Out Producers of 'Kim's Convenience' on Facebook." Toronto Star, June 6, 2021.

DuBois, Macy. Japanese Canadian Cultural Centre: An Appraisal. Toronto: Japanese Canadian Cultural Centre, 1963. Reprinted from The Canadian Architect, March 1964. From the personal collection of Marlene MacKenzie.

Far, Sui Sin. "Leaves from the Mental Portfolio of an Eurasian." Quotidiana. Originally published January 21, 1890. essays. quotidiana.org/far/leaves_mental_portfolio/.

Fihn, Beatrice, and Setsuko Thurlow. "International Campaign to Abolish Nuclear Weapons Nobel Lecture." February 11, 2021, Oslo City Hall. transcript.nobelprize.org/prizes/peace/2017/ican/lecture/.

Final Bow for Yellowface. "About Us." yellowface.org.

Fukushima, Noboru. "The Discourse of Representation — Focusing on Onnagata Actors in Shakespeare's Plays." June 2006. cit.nihon-u.ac.jp/laboratorydata/kenkyu/publication/journal_b/b39.2.pdf.

Goto, Teruji "Tin." Multiple interviews with the author. September 1, 2019.

"Government Apologizes to Japanese Canadians in 1988." CBC Archives, September 22, 1988. cbc.ca/archives/government -apologizes-to-japanese-canadians-in-1988-1.4680546.

Government of Canada. *Cunningham v. Tomey Homma.* canada.ca/en/parks-canada/news/2017/12/cunningham_v_ tomeyhomma.html.

Greenaway, John Endo. "Kokoro Dance: Heart, Soul & Spirit." *The Bulletin/Geppo*, November 1, 2015. jccabulletin-geppo.ca /kokoro-dance-heart-soul-spirit/.

Hadley, Margery. "Oriental Home and School Photos Online." Pacific Mountain Regional Council of The United Church of Canada, April 16, 2016. pacificmountain.ca /oriental-home-and-school-photos-online.

Hall, Millie. "Racial Imposter Syndrome: Finding 'Mixed Race' Belonging Through 'Fake' Racial Identity." NBGA, May 5, 2019. nobasicgirlsallowed.com/racial-imposter-syndrome -finding-mixed-race-belonging-through-fake-racial-identity.

Harding, John S., Victor Sōgen Hori, and Alexander Soucy. *Wild Geese: Buddhism in Canada.* Montreal/Kingston: McGill -Queen's University Press, 2010.

Hartmann, Kathy. Multiple in-person and telephone interviews with the author. September 29, 2019–January 26, 2020.

Hastings Park 1942. "Buildings." Accessed January 16, 2020. hastingspark1942.ca/buildings-overview/livestock-building/.

Hernon, Matthew. "8 Things You Didn't Know About Kyu Sakamoto, the 'Sukiyaki' Singer Who Perished in Japan's Deadliest Plane Crash." *Tokyo Weekender*, August 12, 2020. tokyoweekender.com/2020/08/8-things-you-didnt-know -about-kyu-sakamoto-the-sukiyaki-singer-who-perished-in -japans-deadliest-plane-crash.

Hirabayashi v. United States, 627 F. Supp. 1445 - Dist. Court, WD Washington 1986. scholar.google.ca/scholar_case?case=78520 57775138891482&hl=en&as_sdt=6&as_vis=1 &oi=scholarr.

Hoshiko, Michael S. *Who Was Who: Pioneer Japanese Families in Delta and Surrey*. Marceline, MO: Herff Jones, 1998.

"International Day of Nikkei." Kaigai Nikkeijin Kyokai. June 20, 2019. YouTube video, 1:39. youtube.com/watch?v =aVaLYD8vojg&t=7s.

Japanese Canadian Cultural Centre, Archive and Collections. "Bon Odori Season Approaches." *Japanese Canadian Cultural Centre Newsletter* 16, no. 5 (June/July 1990), 5.

———. "Life in the Canadian Internment and POW Camps." Discover Nikkei. discovernikkei.org/en/nikkeialbum/ albums/6/slide/?page=2.

———. "Nisei Veterans' Award." *Japanese Canadian Cultural Centre Newsletter* 32, no. 8 (June/July/August 2006), 16. yumpu.com/en/document/read/15756505/june-july -japanese-canadian-cultural-centre.

———. *Official Opening of the Japanese Canadian Cultural Centre by The Right Honourable Lester B. Pearson Prime Minister of Canada*. Toronto: Japanese Canadian Cultural Centre, 1964. From the private collection of Marlene MacKenzie.

———. *Salute to 25 Years: 1963–1988*. Japanese Canadian Cultural Centre 25th Anniversary Publication Board. Toronto: Japanese Canadian Cultural Centre, 1988.

———. "Volunteer Awards." jccc.on.ca/join-support/volunteer /volunteer-awards.

Japanese Merchant Ships Recognition Handbook. maritime.org/doc /id/oni208j-japan-merchant-ships/front003.htm.

Japanese Overseas Association. "Background of the Event." jadesas.or
.jp/jp/taikai/.

Javed, Noor. "The Couple Who Put Toronto on the Map." *Toronto
Star*, April 4, 2009. Accessed March 10, 2024. thestar.com
/news/gta/the-couple-who-put-toronto-on-the-map/article
_56d90c02-72a5-5856-9556-e688aecbc828.html.

Jodo Shinshu Buddhist Temples of Canada. "Buddhism in
Canada." jsbtc.ca/jodoshinshu/history.html.

Joya, Mock. *Quaint Customs and Manners of Japan*, vols. 1 & 2.
Tokyo: Tokyo News Service, 1951.

Katsumi, Debbie (née Suyama). Email interviews with the author.
August 18–19 and September 10, 2021.

Kawano, Roland M. *Ministry to the Hopelessly Hopeless: Japanese
Canadian Evacuees and Churches during WWII*. Scarborough,
ON: The Japanese Canadian Christian Churches Historical
Project, 1997.

Keung, Nicholas. "Buddhist Church Rejoices; Parishioners Succeed
in Preserving Their Heritage While Integrating into Canadian
Society Modern New House of Worship, Opening Today,
Testament to 60-Year Effort." *Toronto Star*, August 20, 2005,
Ontario edition.

Kokoro Dance Theatre Society. kokoro.ca.

Lee, Josephine. *The Japan of Pure Invention: Gilbert & Sullivan's
The Mikado*. Minneapolis: University of Minnesota Press,
2010.

———. "Yellowface Performance: Historical and Contemporary
Contexts." *Oxford Research Encyclopedia of Literature*,
February 25, 2019. Accessed August 11, 2020. oxfordre.com
/literature/display/10.1093/acrefore/9780190201098.001.0001
/acrefore-9780190201098-e-834.

"The Legendary Singer Kyu Sakamoto Who Was Gone in a Plane
Accident — Let's Walk Facing Up!" Famous & Popular
Japan, December 4, 2017. famous-popular.tokyo/en/joyful
/entertainment-en/song/1446/.

Loke, Margarett. "Butoh: Dance of Darkness." *New York Times Magazine*, November 1, 1987. nytimes.com/1987/11/01/magazine/butoh-dance-of-darkness.html.

MacKenzie, Marlene. Email interviews with the author. March 6–7, 2020.

Makabe, Tomoko. "No Easy Task Launching Nikkei Voice." *Nikkei Voice* vol. 16, no. 10 (December 2002–January 2003): 1, 13.

McLellan, Janet. *Many Petals of the Lotus: Five Asian Buddhist Communities in Toronto.* Toronto: University of Toronto Press, 1999.

Mesley, Wendy, and Karen Webb. "The National with Peter Mansbridge, Government Apologizes to Japanese Canadians in 1988." CBC, September 22, 1988. CBC Archives video, 4:30. cbc.ca/archives/government-apologizes-to-japanese-canadians-in-1988-1.4680546.

Mori, Ken. "J.C. Centennial Committee Approved 'Canada Ondo' Recording Now on Sale." *New Canadian*, June 3, 1967. From the personal collection of Mark Nishihama.

Motoyoshi, Akiko. *Japanese Phrase Book.* London: BBC Books, 1995.

Mullins, Mark R. "The Organizational Dilemmas of Ethnic Churches: A Case Study of Japanese Buddhism in Canada." *Sociology of Religion* 49, no. 3 (Fall 1988): 217–33.

Nakamura, George. Telephone conversation with the author. October 14, 2021.

Nakamura, Yaeki. Telephone interviews with the author. September 29, 2019, and January–February 2020.

National Association of Japanese Canadians. "BC Redress." Accessed October 25, 2019. bcredress.ca/.

National Association of Japanese Canadians Greater Toronto Chapter. "Premier Horgan's Sin of Omission." Press release, June 10, 2020. torontonajc.ca/2020/06/10/premier-horgans-sin-of-omission/.

Nishihama, Mark. Email interviews with the author. July–October 2020.

Nishimura, Yasuko. Letter of translation to Shigeru Nakamura. March 1982.

Noor Cultural Centre. "The Building." Accessed March 10, 2024. noorculturalcentre.ca/about-2/the-building/.

"Obon Odori Attracts Best Crowd Ever." *Continental Times*, July 14, 1967. From the private collection of Mark Nishihama.

Ohki, Takashi. "Demographic Characteristics of Japanese Canadians in 2016." National Association of Japanese Canadians. najc.ca/wp-content/uploads/2018/05/2016-Census-Japanese-Canadians-Eng-Final.pdf.

Omatsu, Maryka, writer/producer. *Swimming Upstream: Japanese Canadian Struggle for Justice in BC*. Toronto: The Canadian Race Relations Foundation, 2018.

Orde Street School: 100 Years of History. 2015. "Heritage, Education, and Planning: The Orde Street School Building." ordestreetschool100.blogspot.com/?view=classic.

Otsuka, Julie. *The Buddha in the Attic*. Farmington Hills, MI: Thorndike Press, 1995.

Ozeki, Ruth. *The Face: A Time Code*. Amherst, MA: Restless Books, 2015.

"Past Trauma May Haunt Your Future Health." Harvard Health Publishing, February 12, 2021. health.harvard.edu/diseases-and-conditions/past-trauma-may-haunt-your-future-health.

Payne, Laura. "Izumo no Okuni: The Woman Who Created Kabuki." *GaijinPot* (blog), June 12, 2023. Accessed March 10, 2024. blog.gaijinpot.com/izumo-no-okuni-the-woman-who-created-kabuki/.

Pruner, Yoshimi. Email interviews with the author. December 5–8, 2021.

Reid, Susan. "Congregation Fights Sale of Church." *Toronto Star*, June 24, 1991.

Rexroth, Kenneth. *One Hundred Poems from the Japanese*. New York: New Directions, 1955.

Richman-Abdou, Kelly. "Kintsugi: The Centuries-Old Art of Repairing Broken Pottery with Gold." My Modern Met, September 5, 2019. mymodernmet.com/kintsugi-kintsukuroi/.

Richwine, Lisa. "Study Finds Asians Largely 'Invisible' in Hollywood's Top Films." Reuters, May 19, 2021. reuters.com /lifestyle/study-finds-asians-largely-invisible-hollywoods-top -films-2021-05-18/.

Root, Maria P.P. "A Bill of Rights for Racially Mixed People." In *The Multiracial Experience: Racial Borders as the New Frontier*, edited by Maria P. P. Root, 3–14. Thousand Oaks, CA: Sage, 1996.

"Sansei Choir Seeks More New Members." *Continental Times*, October 11, 1966. From the private collection of Mark Nishihama.

Sherrow, Victoria. *Encyclopedia of Hair: A Cultural History*. Westport, CT: Greenwood Press, 2006.

Sison, Marites "Tess." "Japan Trip Highlights Canadian Connections." *Anglican Journal*, September 11, 2012. Accessed October 28, 2019. anglican.ca/news/japan-trip-highlights -canadian-connections/300466/.

Sugiman, Pamela. "Passing Time, Moving Memories: Interpreting Wartime Narratives of Japanese Canadian Women." *Histoire sociale/Social History* 37, no. 73 (2004): 78–79. hssh.journals .yorku.ca/index.php/hssh/article/view/4374.

Takata, Toyo. *Nikkei Legacy: The Story of Japanese Canadians from Settlement to Today*. Toronto: New Canada Publications, 1983.

Teruya, Roberto Oshiro. "International Nikkei Day — June 20, 2018." Translated by Kora McNaughton. Discover Nikkei, July 31, 2018. discovernikkei.org/en/journal/2018/7/31/dia -internacional-nikkei.

Toronto Buddhist Church. "A Jodo Shinshu Temple Located in Toronto." Accessed September 17, 2019. tbc.on.ca/.

———. "Obon." Accessed March 10, 2024. tbc.on.ca/join-us /special-observances-services/.

Toronto Creative Music Lab. "About." tcml-admin.squarespace.com.

Toronto Japanese Language School. *Ayumi: Toronto Japanese Language School Fortieth Anniversary 1949–1989*.

———. "Welcome to the Toronto Japanese Language School." tjls.ca.

Tory, John. "Japanese Canadian Freedom Day." Facebook, April 1, 2021. facebook.com/photo/?fbid=10165350969310495&set =a.10150175732745495.

"The 12 Laws of Karma Everyone Should Know!" Happy Buddha. beinghappybuddha.com/blogs/insights/the-12-laws -of-karma-everyone-should-know.

Wakisaka, Amy. Email interview with the author. November 1, 2019.

Wallin, Lisa. "Nihongami: Japanese Hairstyles Through the Ages." *Tokyo Weekender*, January 10, 2018. tokyoweekender.com/2018/01/nihongami-japanese-hairstyles -through-the-ages/.

Watada, Terry. *Bukkyo Tozen: A History of Jodo Shinshu Buddhism in Canada 1905–1995.* Toronto: Toronto Buddhist Church, 1996.

Weir, Kirsten. "Feel Like a Fraud?" *GradPsych*, November 2013. apa.org/gradpsych/2013/11/fraud.

Wertheim, Jon. "Kabuki: Inside the Japanese Artform with Its Biggest Star, Ebizo." *60 Minutes.* CBS News, April 19, 2020. cbsnews .com/news/kabuki-japanese-theater-art-make-up-dances-ebizo -60-minutes-2020-12-27/.

"What Is Nikkei?" Discover Nikkei. discovernikkei.org/en/about /what-is-nikkei.

Wilson, Rev. Joan. Email interview. October 28, 2019.

IMAGE CREDITS

ADDITIONAL CREDITS

"The Kimono" was previously published in *Nikkei Voice* in July/August 2004.

An excerpt from "Odori Primer" was previously published in the quarterly newsletter of the Toronto Chapter of the National Association of Japanese Canadians in December 1999.

An excerpt from "Miss Tokyo" was previously published in *Return*, issue 01, July 2021.

• • •

Excerpts from *The Enemy That Never Was*, by Ken Adachi, © 1991 Estate of Ken Adachi. Used with permission.

Excerpts from *Contemporary Directions in Asian American Dance*, edited by Yutian Wong. Reprinted by permission of the University of Wisconsin Pres. © 2018 by the Board of Regents of the University of Wisconsin System. All rights reserved.

Quotes by Jay Hirabayashi, from *The Bulletin/Geppo* November 2015 issue, © Greater Vancouver Japanese Canadian Citizens' Association. Used with permission.

Excerpt from "Oriental Home and School Photos Online" © Margery Hadley. Used with permission.

Excerpts from *Wild Geese: Buddhism in Canada* © 2010 John S. Harding, Victor Sōgen Hori, Alexander Soucy. Used with permission.

Excerpts from "Passing Time, Moving Memories: Interpreting Wartime Narratives of Japanese Canadian Women," by

ABOUT THE AUTHOR

SUZANNE ELKI YOKO HARTMANN is a fourth-generation Japanese Canadian with German ancestry. The editor, writer, and self-published children's book author (*My Father's Nose*, 2016) began her media career in the wilds of television at Citytv and then the CBC before she sidestepped to print, web, and digital. Her work has been featured in *Vitality*, *Style at Home*, *Canadian Living*, and the *Toronto Star*.

Active in the Japanese Canadian community, Suzanne divides her time as a board member between the Toronto chapter of the National Association of Japanese Canadians (Toronto NAJC) and Toronto Japanese Garden Club.

The self-described word nerd holds a master of fine arts in creative nonfiction from University of King's College, a certificate in magazine publishing, and a bachelor's degree in radio & television arts from Toronto Metropolitan University.

Her MFA project was awarded the NAJC Endowment Fund's 2020 SEAD grant and selected for the 2021 BIPOC Writers Connect mentorship conference hosted by the Writers' Union of Canada. She also received a 2022 writer's grant from the Toronto Arts Council to complete the work. She lives with her family and dog in Toronto.